CW00472380

Dark Angels On Writing

Dark Angels On Writing

Changing Lives with Words

The Dark Angels Collective

unbound

This edition first published in 2019

Unbound
6th Floor Mutual House, 70 Conduit Street, London W1S 2GF
www.unbound.com
All rights reserved

© John Simmons (editor), 2019
© Neil Baker, Claire Bodanis, Gillian Colhoun, Stuart Delves, Mike Gogan,
Jamie Jauncey, Martin Lee, Elen Lewis, Andy Milligan, Richard Pelletier,
John Simmons, Craig B. Watson (individual contributors), 2019

The right of the Dark Angels Collective to be identified as the author of this
work has been asserted in accordance with Section 77 of the Copyright,
Designs and Patents Act 1988. No part of this publication may be copied,
reproduced, stored in a retrieval system, or transmitted, in any form or by
any means without the prior permission of the publisher, nor be otherwise
circulated in any form of binding or cover other than that in which it is
published and without a similar condition being imposed on the subsequent
purchaser.

ISBN (eBook): 978-1-78965-044-0
ISBN (Paperback): 978-1-78965-043-3

Cover design by Mecob

Printed and bound in Great Britain by Clays Ltd, Elcograf S.p.A.

MIX
Paper from
responsible sources
FSC® C018072
www.fsc.org

To all Dark Angels – past, present and future

Super patrons

Lisa Andrews
Nick Asbury
Heather Atchison
Kate Baxter
Josiane Bonieux
Ken Burnett
David Cameron
Ezri Carlebach
Iain Carruthers
Stuart Clark
Gillian Colhoun
Jon Copestake
Quentin Crowe
Rishi Dastidar
Brian Davidson
John Dodds
James T. Doyle
Sarah Ellis
Bret Feddern
Sam Fitzpatrick
Michael Gough
Jeremy Hill
Steve & Sarah Hill
Gill Hodge
Anita Holford
Tim Horrox
Douglas Howatt
Jules James

The James Hutton Institute
Ian Kelly
Dan Kieran
Therese Kieran
Frances Leavy
Jean & Alun Lewis
Johnny Lyons
Gráinne Mac Giolla Rí
Jeannie Maclean
Brian Mcleish
Andy Milligan
John Mitchinson
Michelle Nicol
Mark Noad
Nick Parker
Justin Pollard
Ed Prichard
Paul Redstone
Jane Reeve
Erica Reid
Fiona Ritchie
Mark Roberts
Rowena Roberts
Andy Sanwell
The Sharp End
Faye Sharpe
Tara Simpson
Teresa Smith
Ashvin Sologar
Stephen Swindley
Dominic Varley
Giles Watkins
Elissa Watson

Jacob Watson
Judith Watson
Karen Whitaker
Alison Woolven

Contents

PART IV.
STAYING TRUE TO YOURSELF

About this book

In 2003 three writers came together for an event at the Edinburgh International Book Festival: John Simmons, whose book was its subject; Stuart Delves, who was an advocate for John's work and sponsored the event; and Jamie Jauncey, who chaired it.

That coming together of writers led to Dark Angels. The idea was to provide a different kind of 'training', particularly for writers in the world of business and branding. This was based on the belief that, for business writing to be effective, it needed to be more human. It needed to connect people one to one as individuals, something the often robotic-sounding voices of corporations never seemed to achieve.

Why Dark Angels? These ideas were expressed in John's book of that name. With a nod to Milton's *Paradise Lost* and Philip Pullman's *His Dark Materials*, it referred to human creativity.

So the three writers began running residential courses in remote places, far from the hurly-burly of daily business life. People came, joined in the exercises that stretched intellectual and imaginative muscles and left asking for more. They were copywriters, marketing people, managers and leaders, freelancers – anyone who needed to use words at work; in a word, everyone.

They all asked 'what next?' So we developed courses on three levels – Foundation, Advanced, Masterclass – in places that stimulated stories. Dark Angels became a community of writers, connected by a commitment to better writing in work and life. The courses always contained personal writing alongside business writing, because we believed that each informed the other on the journey towards improvement.

Could all this continue and even grow? In 2015 the founders reached out, as our American alumni put it, and three became twelve. The twelve associate partners were united by their belief in our founding principles: that writing is a life-enriching activity, that writing well leads to greater effectiveness in all aspects of life, that stories are the way human beings best engage with each other. We had seen people transformed by our courses, and the evidence of Dark Angels writers achieving commercial and literary success was growing.

And so Dark Angels became a company that now offers more courses, activities and books. We are finding new locations in the USA, Ireland, Europe, New Zealand, as well as our tried and tested places. The response of participants is as enthusiastic as ever, so we are now planning more courses involving all the new associates. We are experimenting with new formats while staying true to the Dark Angels philosophy.

It was time to capture the philosophy and practice in a book told in the voices of the writers. This book contains chapters written by the twelve associates on aspects of writing that matter most to them: aspects on which they are experts. It also includes a selection of writing by Dark Angels alumni.

We simply invite you to read. We hope this book will stimulate your desire to become a better writer, and help you achieve that aim.

If you wish to find out more about Dark Angels, visit our website www.dark-angels.org.uk. There you will discover more about the courses available and about our backgrounds and origins. We would love to hear from you.

The Dark Angels Collective

Foreword

I am fond of asking my professional colleagues to 'bring themselves to work'. Not to remedy absenteeism, but to benefit from who they really are.

When at work, we all play-act, to varying degrees. We wear different masks, depending on who we're with, or where we are. And business environments seem to be the place in which we assume the most inauthentic version of our true selves.

From our 'work clothes', to the words we speak and write, our business selves assume personas that most of our partners, parents or friends would find unrecognisable, if not hilarious.

In a world in which we are all, in some way, serving a customer or client who themselves are no doubt play-acting as well, isn't it time we just started being ourselves?

Authenticity, sadly, is not easy. Business convention has sullied our noble language, left us 'reaching out' to people and 'reaching in' to opportunities – like a horrific linguistic hokey cokey. In your personal life, how often do you use words such as paradigm, granularity, leverage or Kool-Aid?

In 2004, three enterprising wordsmiths – John Simmons, Stuart Delves and Jamie Jauncey – decided enough was enough. So, instead of running anything up a flagpole or pushing so much as an envelope, they founded Dark Angels – a mission to help people find their true inner voices, and to use those inner voices to change the way they write at work.

And so they came. Disciples from every kind of business, organisation and brand came to attend Dark Angels training courses in beautiful corners of Scotland, Spain and Oxford. Exhausted by years of penning pompous syntax, they were gently and artfully unburdened of their business speak. Day by day, their syllable and word counts shrank, as the potency and warmth of their language blossomed.

People who never considered themselves writers discovered we are in fact all writers. Powerful words were written. Tears were shed. Wine was taken. The Dark Angels philosophy caught on quickly, its concept wonderfully simple but speaking to a universal need.

John, Stuart and Jamie brought the gift of authentic writing to ever-increasing numbers through their courses, articles and business-based training. However, their ambition was much greater, their desire to liberate an even greater number of people even stronger.

And that's where this book comes in.

Between these covers lie the Dark Angels' secrets to better business writing. Oh, let's drop the pretence... this is actually about better writing, full stop. As well as the original three wise men, a number of notable Dark Angel disciples detail their own insights, tricks and tools on the joy and art of writing simply and truly.

This book is so much more than a 'how to' guide. It is a window into a world free of the meaningless words and phrases we have accumulated in life and business. Its lesson is simple but challenging. The road to stronger language lies in reduction and authenticity.

The truth really does lie within.

John Allert
Chief Marketing Officer
McLaren Technology Group

The Foundations

1

What I do isn't what I've always done, which is what I like about it.

Once I just wrote, but then I started to help others write better.

Once I had ideas, and now I work hard to find people who have better ideas than me.

I guess you could say that I've slipped away from working on my craft.

But who says it was my craft in the first place?

I only started writing by accident.

But oh, what a great accident.

Dan Germain, former head of creative at innocent,
now working at Apple

MAKING CONNECTIONS

JOHN SIMMONS

Look yourself in the mirror and ask yourself a question. It can be any question. What's certain is that you will answer it by using words.

Let's assume your question goes beyond the everyday 'What's for breakfast?'. Perhaps it's a question about yourself as a person and about your own life. 'Why do I do what I do?', for instance. It's a question we as writers should ask frequently of ourselves, of our own individual purpose, much as we might question the purpose of the brands or organisations that we deal with. Otherwise you are doing things out of habit rather than conviction.

A writer needs to write from conviction. I write because I love writing; there's no other time when I feel quite as alive as when I'm writing. If I'm lucky, if the words are flowing, time passes almost unnoticed. I find it strange that we can be most in love with life when we're least aware of time – yet working life revolves around limitations set by time. Is this why we often rebel against the routine of 'work' and, as writers, achieve our best work outside those limitations? We become rebels. Dark Angels came from a rebellion against the standard, the formulaic in life and work, and we use words as instruments of rebellion. Because, as we often say on our courses, we see no reason for writing to be boring.

This comes from a belief in the power of words. Words tap into our emotions, memories and imaginations, if they are used well. They appear on the page and the screen ready for further shaping. It's a process that gives me joy, even exhilaration; that stirs me enough to bring tears to my eyes at times. If so, I know the chances are that the reader will connect with those feelings and share them. The reader will feel engaged and curious because the writer is; will smile from a shared insight; will well up at the connection to a personal feeling that is also universal. *Only connect.*

Yes, I'm talking about writing fiction. And, yes, I'm also talking about business writing. Both of them need writers and readers who communicate better with each other through stories they recognise as containing fundamental truths.

That's something I've known, if not always articulated, all through my working life. This book is my attempt, along with other like-minded writers, to show why this approach works.

Let me go back to my writing at work. People credit me with 'inventing' tone of voice, which is gratifying in one sense; but I'm not sure I want to accept the credit when I see a lot of the work produced under its banner. Coming from the world of branding I'd always thought of it as a means for a brand to differentiate itself through the words it uses. That was certainly my starting point, first at Newell and Sorrell, then at Interbrand. I was working with some big and famous brands, and they all wanted to stand out from the crowd, to build loyalty among their audiences, to create the affection that would keep people returning to them as customers.

I was fortunate to be working with brands that I liked. For example, Waterstone's with their love of books in the 1990s, Guinness with its communion (their word) with the mysteries of their product. They were brands that lent themselves easily to storytelling and that had a respect for words. The question I kept asking – 'How do brands communicate if they don't use words?' – was easily understood by them. Of course brands need words.

In the case of Waterstone's (who recently dropped the apostrophe from their brand name) this was demonstrated through marketing and promotional programmes, particularly in stores, that were built around words. The most common exchange between shop and customer at the time was the carrier bag, your way to carry away books purchased. It seemed we really needed to do more than stamp the logo on the bags, so we saw them as a way to show the connection Waterstone's made between books and readers. A whole range of carrier bags used quotations, with a verbal device 'Books to…' that linked the quotation to the purpose of reading. My first choice was the E. M. Forster epigraph from *Howards End*: 'Only connect'. *Books to make connections at Waterstone's.* It was then, and remains now, a mantra for life and writing.

Guinness took me closer to the heart of storytelling. It seems now that every brand has discovered 'storytelling' – but without always properly understanding it, and often without the ability to tell a story well. With Guinness – a brand that surely deserves the word 'iconic' – I was brought in to research and tell the stories that would demonstrate the newly agreed brand essence of 'inner strength'. There were many that I wrote for an internal book to be used by the global marketing teams, but my favourite is still the founding story about Arthur Guinness. Founding stories are powerful for all brands.

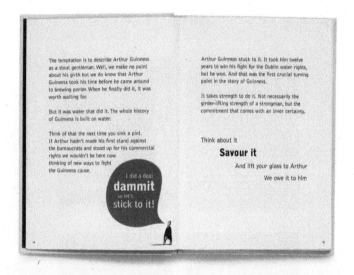

The temptation is to describe Arthur Guinness as a stout gentleman. Well, we make no point about his girth but we do know that Arthur Guinness took his time before he came around to brewing porter. When he finally did it, it was worth waiting for.

But it was water that did it. The whole history of Guinness is built on water.

Think of that the next time you sink a pint. If Arthur hadn't made his first stand against the bureaucrats and stood up for his commercial rights we wouldn't be here now thinking of new ways to fight the Guinness cause.

I did a deal **dammit** so let's stick to it!

Arthur Guinness stuck to it. It took him twelve years to win his fight for the Dublin water rights, but he won. And that was the first crucial turning point in the story of Guinness.

It takes strength to do it. Not necessarily the girder-lifting strength of a strongman, but the commitment that comes with an inner certainty.

Think about it

Savour it

And lift your glass to Arthur

We owe it to him

This story was effectively rediscovered. It had fallen out of corporate memory. Its rediscovery had a galvanising effect on a new wave of Guinness marketing activity, including the institution of 17:59 emails. These communications to the global team began as a nod towards the founding date, 1759, but then referred to the time on the clock that marked the end of the week on a Friday evening – and time for a reflection on the week passed and the week to come.

It's clear from these examples that brands can use words and stories in ways to differentiate themselves. Partly as a result of such examples, brands started incorporating 'tone of voice' into the tools they could use to set themselves apart from the competition – all well and good. Other examples – perhaps innocent smoothies, most famously – started to use words with wit and purpose. Innocent has grown from its origins in a Shepherd's Bush shed, when I first wrote about them, to a multinational company owned by Coca-Cola, that still loves the words that appear on its packaging. And now those words, as I discovered when running a workshop recently at Fruit Towers, are written in French, German, Russian, Finnish and many other languages, while remaining true to the brand.

That's not easy. What is easy, but not necessarily right, is to imitate innocent. It's a brand that has spawned thousands of imitators, and many of them are inappropriate. I'll accept cheekiness from my fruit drink but not from my accountants. Words need to be chosen with care to fit the brand they are written for.

One local example, a small business that does it well while creating its own personality, is Prohibition Wines in Muswell Hill. They might not take over the world from a north London suburb but their fame is spreading among the local community, thanks to the wit of their words. Paul Shanley writes the words and owned the business that he set up (recently selling it for a good price to Jeroboams). This was an unintended effect of one of my workshops, attended by Paul as a participant from London University's SOAS. Inspired by the potential and fun of words to describe a business, he left the academic world and became a wine-seller.

Dear Prohibitionists

This week has been all about confronting our irrational fears. In order to try to move away from seeing blue tits through a Daphne du Maurier lens, Mr Prohibition Wines went to hang out with 130 small birds in one of the London Zoo aviaries, telling himself that a few birds were hardly going to bring about the end of the world. At least one of our customers spotted him looking shifty but at least no-one heard him screaming and he finally appears to be getting over his bird phobia (*newsletters passim*). And no one asked him if he wanted to buy a monkey. Mrs Prohibition wines on the other hand decided to do some work on her chronic fear of hazy, double hopped, double IPAs which is why this newsletter is somewhat later than it should be.

I enjoy reading the weekly news from Prohibition and it entices me to their shop. They make the necessary connection. You might argue that this is easier to do when you're a small business than a large one, but that really sets out the challenge. There is no reason why interesting words should work less well for a bigger brand. Sometimes the big brands rise like fireworks then fade from the scene – Orange, for example – but often the fade is caused by a bigger company acquiring them and not fully understanding what it has acquired, including the language assets of the brand.

Most brands now include tone of voice in their marketing repertoire, ticking it off as a must-have without really striving for the distinctiveness that could make the brand more famous. There has been a raising of standards, but most brands have stopped at the foothills of the climb. Many years ago Boots, the high-street chemist, defined its tone as 'clear, warm and fresh', which moved its use of language to something more human and interactive. Many other brands since could be defined as 'clear, warm and fresh'. I have no wish to argue against the merits of clarity, warmth and freshness in language but there is little sense of challenge in the description. It takes a brand close to the Plain English Campaign, but few of us like to be described as plain. What more could you do?

There are interesting examples: J. Peterman, Monzo, onefinestay. But I hesitate to set down firm guidelines, knowing that tone of voice can be a fragile flower, sustained by the care of an individual or small group of champions. They need encouragement – from their colleagues and managers – and they need training. Training should not be the schooling of people in the rote learning of 'only do it like this'. I always prefer the Nordstrom advice: 'Use best judgement in all situations. There will be no additional rules.' But to use judgement and initiative people need confidence and support, and they need practice in writing in different ways, not all of which will be obviously applicable to the immediate tasks at their place of work.

I always think of Joni Mitchell's answer when asked about her own songwriting practice: 'I always like harder puzzles.' The trick is to solve the puzzle so that it looks effortless and natural, and in a way that takes the development of skills through playfulness. In my first book, *We, Me, Them & It*, I quoted Douglas R. Hofstadter, whose words had been a moment of sudden illumination for me: 'I suspect that the welcoming of constraints is, at bottom, the deepest secret of creativity.'

It then became clear to me, through my own writing at work, through the books I wrote about writing and through the Dark Angels courses that I was running, that constraints do liberate a writer creatively. There is something about setting a constraint – word count, the number of syllables (as in a haiku), the use of different letters to begin or end words, the development of a particular form (as in poetry) – that challenges our brains to accept yet find a way around the obstacle raised. Time after time in workshops I have seen the truth of this: writers respond to the challenge of a constraint. And indeed there is nothing new in this – for example, briefs containing word counts have been around in advertising, journalism and copywriting since these crafts were first practised. It works.

But the more interesting and challenging constraints work even better. They encourage a writer to discover that 'there's always another way of writing something'. Often that other way is better, but the important thing for a writer is to explore, and have fun in the exploration. It liberates you from the shackles of corporate language, which falls back only too easily into the tropes of managerial-speak and jargon. We all come across examples daily. This morning I listened to the CEO of Sky talking on the radio about 'optionality' as in 'we offer customers greater optionality' – because, presumably, he believes 'greater optionality' makes him sound more of a business leader than 'more options' or even 'greater choice'. I think it makes him sound more like a robot than a human being, and humanity is the quality I look for most of all in writing.

All writers need to feel empathy. This is a quality that comes naturally but can also be developed through writing fiction, where obviously the writer is creating character and trying to elicit some kind of emotional response. I recommend that business writers develop their own writing through writing fiction. Apart from anything else it gives great pleasure to the writer, who learns not only empathy but all the other elements of writing, including choice of words, rhythm, dialogue and, for me increasingly importantly, structure.

But business writing is what most readers of this book will do for their living, and it's a form of writing that we should take pride in. What higher calling can a piece of commercial work achieve than to live beyond the 'buy me' message of its origins and gain a place in our collective memory? For example, down the years Guinness advertising has staked its place for posterity so that, almost a century later, we all recall 'Guinness is good for you' even though the brand has not used that line during the lifetimes of most of its customers.

We live now in a world of social media, whose tone is driven by conversation. Much as we might have reservations about aspects of Facebook and Twitter, we have come to rely on them and the mobile phones that deliver them. They use constraints, of course, that encourage you towards a conversational style and a more compressed form of language. These are the imperatives of twenty-first-century communication. But they do not rule out craft, precision and playfulness. Those are qualities to admire and hone through practice. They help us connect better with others – which might be a reasonable definition of 'marketing', a discipline that works at its best when it remembers its human values.

So my advice is to stretch yourself with writing exercises that put you in touch with your deeper feelings and that encourage you to take risks with words. These are exercises, after all; they are not for you to publicly display – unless you choose to do so. It's not about writing poetry in an annual report, though it could be about using skills learned from poetry to make a more interesting report. It's not about inventing a myth to communicate your business to the world, although it might be about writing a myth to better understand the purpose of what you do. It's not about writing haikus to put into emails, but to hone your editing and vocabulary skills; to be more playful with words so that you avoid writing that is stale – writing that is unappetising because it is stale. Make it fresh for yourself and you will make it fresh for your readers.

You need to work on this, and those of you who have been on a Dark Angels course will have a good understanding of what is needed. But we all need to seek out opportunities and fresh challenges that will keep improving our writing. Write daily in a notebook, carry notebooks with you everywhere; writing by hand works better for me for first drafts and notes, but we will each develop our own best practices. Use your notebook for recording and developing ideas.

I can't understand why people are frightened of new ideas. I'm frightened of the old ones.

John Cage, composer

Seek creative challenges through writing groups so that you can share writing. As well as projects arising from Dark Angels, I recommend the writers' group 26. I declare an interest as one of its co-founders, but it's nevertheless true that 26 has been creating partnerships since 2003 with organisations that lead to stimulating challenges. These have involved major institutions like the V&A, National Museum of Scotland, Platform for Art, British Library and Imperial War Museums. Sometimes they lead to new forms such as the sestude – 26 in reflection, using exactly 62 words – or the centena, marking the centenary of the First World War in 100 words, of which the first three are repeated as the last three. They work.

I'll close with a final example: 26 worked with an organisation of calligraphers and typographers called Letter Exchange. Individual writers selected words by inserting a knife into the *Oxford English Dictionary* and seeing what they landed on. Twenty-six words were chosen, one to represent each letter of the alphabet. Each writer then worked with a designer/calligrapher to produce a work inspired by that word, and some beautiful pieces resulted.

I was assigned all twenty-six of these randomly chosen words and asked to combine them into one work. There were some arcane words in there, so I needed to look them up in the dictionary; but there was a very familiar, reassuring one in 'connected', which was wonderfully serendipitous. I put all the words together to make a poem that made some sense, and allowed me to express 'Only connect' in my own way. *Everything is connected.*

The *battement* of the present beats on,
undulates into the future, with a
dismissive *wave* towards the past.

We light upon *fractions* of history,
touchwood creatures burning off
the memories of cultures not our own:
Yankton, Scythic, Vinča.

We reveal the remains of lives we *acidulate*
with our uncomprehending *glance.*
We *dig*, we excavate, we make *ordination*
beneath rock and desert and *quag*

miring ourselves in *rash*
assumptions of hostile difference
when really these are *mates* leaving
us strangers a misunderstood *xenium.*

Meanwhile out at sea the *porpoise* leaps
and on land the *kangaroo* hops
while we wear *jeans* and trainers
lacking poise to make our *excusation*.

The *hearse* of history edges forward,
the *naviculoid* burial vessel sets sail.
Yet sometimes and sudden an *inpouring*
of feeling creates the vivid picture

as if cut out of *lino*
and coloured in *zaffre*,
a bright image to say:
Everything is *connected*.

Will this kind of writing improve your writing at work?
Definitely.

Try this

Randomly choose three words from a dictionary. Insert a knife
in the dictionary to make your choice, noting the words that it
points at.

Then take a paragraph from a piece of writing at work – one
that could be improved. See what happens when you rewrite it
using one or all three of the words.

2

Growing up in our household, a treacherous gap would sometimes open between words and truth. The voices said one thing, our hearts heard another. In the asylum of my bedroom, books were windows onto other places, other lives. I learned to open those windows; to climb in and out. And then I learned to write, so I could help the people back home understand each other. So I could understand myself.

Misunderstanding limits us – as individuals, families, businesses, communities. Writing can liberate by uniting our mind with our soul; our needs with our joy; our self with society. Words can draw maps of common ground and invite us to light out for new territory. Words can also lay inviting pathways to a place beyond language – but that's another story.

Each day, to connect and explore through language – to offer windows onto the as-yet unthought, unfelt, unimagined – what a life!

Tim Rich, writer and communications consultant

FIRE IN THE CAVE

JAMIE JAUNCEY

In every bit of honest writing in the world ... there is a base theme. Try to understand men, if you understand each other you will be kind to each other. Knowing a man well never leads to hate and nearly always leads to love.

John Steinbeck

A few days before Christmas 1994, three cave scientists were working their way along the side of the Ardèche River gorge in southern France, looking for air vents that might betray the presence of cave systems. Their attention was drawn to a rockfall, partially concealed by vegetation.

They pulled away the debris until they had made a hole large enough to wriggle through. Switching on their headlamps, they clambered down into a cave. The air was dead and stale, the darkness intense. They moved cautiously forward, making their way deeper and deeper into a network of passages and chambers.

They had gone some distance when one pointed ahead to a figure that had become visible on the rock, clearly illuminated in the beam of his headlamp. It was the head of a horse, represented with extraordinary accuracy and beauty, its eyes wide, nostrils flared and mouth open in an almost audible whinny.

The further they went the more paintings they found. There were mammoths and woolly rhinoceroses, deer and bison, cave-dwelling lions, bears and hyenas, a panther and, one of only two representations of the human form, the handprints of a man with a crooked little finger. This glittering, stalactite-filled art gallery was a pristine time capsule. For 30,000 years it had been sealed and perfectly preserved by the limestone cliff that had collapsed across its mouth.

Everywhere in the images the impression of movement was heightened by the artists' use of the natural contours of the cave walls. The whinnying horse was one of a group in apparent conversation. Elsewhere, two rhinoceroses were locked in combat. A lioness bared her teeth at the amorous advances of a male. A bison took flight, along with a galloping aurochs.

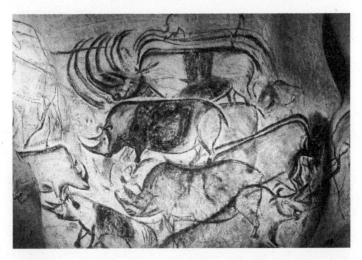

And in the dust on the cave floor were the footprints of a boy, with those of a wolf following him. Were they companions? Was the boy the wolf's intended prey? Or had they walked the cave in different eras, separated by a gulf in time?

The full story of the Chauvet Cave is told by the film-maker Werner Herzog in his mesmerising documentary, *Cave of Forgotten Dreams*. It's a tale of the very origins of story itself.

We will never know how the battle between the two rhinoceroses ended, nor what had frightened the fleeing bison. We can only guess at the memories those ancient hunters relived as they gazed at the scenes by the flickering light of a torch, or the warnings they gave their children: don't go near such-and-such a place, a cave lion lives there, see how fierce he looks. And we can only imagine what part the paintings played in their rituals, their invocations and appeasements.

But these delicate, exquisite works of art serve as compelling early evidence that *Homo sapiens* is, above almost everything else, a storytelling species.

Our ability to conceive of otherness – that is to say, to imagine – is one of the defining characteristics of our kind. As those early cave painters knew, stories get us in the imagination, the place where heart and mind come together. They may amuse and delight us, but they also move us, tell us important things, help us make sense of the world and sometimes change the way we see it. Why else is it that storytellers are among the first to be singled out by authoritarian regimes?

By inviting us to see the world through lenses other than our own, stories foster empathy; they connect us with ourselves as well as with others. This is why, for example, fiction-reading programmes in prisons have been so effective in helping to prepare offenders for re-entry into society. Terrence Gargiulo, an American management consultant and storyteller, says simply, 'The shortest distance between two people is a story.'

Neuroscientists also take a keen interest in the way stories work on us. Researchers at Princeton University invited a volunteer to undergo an fMRI scan while telling a simple story about her recent daily life. As she did so they recorded her voice and measured her brain activity. Several other volunteers then underwent a similar scan while listening to the playback of the story. The researchers found that identical parts of the brain lit up in the teller and the listener.

That wasn't all. They noted that the more closely in sync the teller's and listeners' brain patterns, the better recall of the story the listener had. And as the story unfolded, some listeners' brain activity indicated that they were anticipating the teller; in other words, they were doing what we all do when being told a story – guessing how it was going to turn out.

Contrary to long-held belief, we now know that decision-making takes place not in the neocortex, the frontal part of the brain which controls analytical thinking and cognition, but in the amygdala, the ancient, almond-shaped part of the brain where emotion and feelings register (the neocortex being simply where we rationalise these decisions after the event). It follows, then, that since stories reach our emotions, they also tend to have more influence on our thought processes than mere facts.

In Oxford, the evolutionary psychologist Robin Dunbar notes that 60 per cent of our daily conversation takes the form of stories or anecdotes. And we are known to be many times more likely to retain information, and to process it more deeply, when it is conveyed in a story than in, say, a series of numbered points.

But what is a story?

In his collection *365 Stories*, the Scottish novelist James Robertson writes: 'A writer friend tells me that if he said he went on a train from Perth to Doncaster, changing at Edinburgh, that wouldn't be a story, but if he said that it was only when he got to Doncaster that he realised he'd left his bag in Edinburgh, that would be. Something has to change for it to

be a story, my friend the writer said, something has to happen.'
(The friend, I should declare, is me.)

Shawn Callahan of Australian storytelling agency Anecdote
maintains in his book, *Putting Stories to Work*, that stories need
certain ingredients. They must have real people doing real
things; characters with names; a time marker; a place marker;
and something unexpected. He goes on to describe the classic
story structure as follows: in the past... then something
happened... so now... in the future... There are many
formulations of this, but they all contain the critical element of
reversal or challenge or conflict, without which there would be
no story.

As a writer of fiction, and therefore someone who is used
to spending part of his time in an imagined world, I apply
these basic principles of storytelling instinctively, inhaled as
they were from the pages of the novels into which I retreated
as a child, even before boarding school rendered that escape a
necessity rather than a simple pleasure.

Today, story remains the most powerful tool at my disposal
whatever I happen to be writing. As professional writers of
every stripe – novelists, biographers, journalists, copywriters
and many others – know, story is the engine, the energy-giver
of all writing. And one of its great powers is the fact that it
asks nothing more of its audience than to listen and to feel. Fact
or fiction, a well-told story in which we engage fully with the
protagonists and their dilemmas carries us along on a current
of emotion. It does not require us to respond or act, to agree
or disagree, to analyse or reflect; and if we do, we do so on our
own terms, not according to instructions given.

Yet here is the paradox: whenever we hear or read a story,
any story, we are changed by it in some minute or subtle way.
Every story carries a subtext, an ulterior motive, conscious or
subconscious, on the part of the teller; something that goes

beyond the intention simply to entertain or inform. It's human nature to encode messages, after all – just think of Aesop. And we, as readers or listeners, are susceptible to those messages.

Shortly before the opening ceremony of the 2012 London Olympics, the director Danny Boyle ran a dress rehearsal to which all 70,000 volunteers were invited. Secrecy was all-important, but with such a large number of people, the risks of someone giving the game away were high. Before the show, Boyle addressed the crowd and told them how much their contribution to the Games was valued. He then implored them not to breathe a word of what they were about to see. In the event there was not a single leak. The volunteers were unpaid. G4S, meanwhile, which had been awarded a £280 million contract to provide security staff for the Games, abjectly failed to deliver on its promise and the army had to be called in.

And the point? Aesop might simply have concluded that if you are good to people they will be good to you; or, that no amount of money will turn a lame horse into a winner. The point is that there is always a point.

Stories travel like water. Once told they can no more be contained than they can be untold. Organisations like to control the information that flows out of and around them, so there is a certain tension in the way businesses and institutions approach story. They are intrigued by it, they recognise its power, but they are at the same time a little fearful of it. Since all stories turn on challenge or reversal, organisations have to own up to their own challenges, even failures, despite the preferred business story being one in which the graph continues to rise smoothly and steadily (which, in itself, is the story of our modern obsession with growth).

Having said that, there are increasing numbers of organisations today that see storytelling as the glue that holds them together. These are the brands that know how stories not only draw their customers into their cultural and emotional orbits, but also help staff to connect with one another and find a common sense of purpose. These organisations know that stories are the best way to capture and store knowledge, to understand and manage change, to define and encourage good leadership. These are the organisations that don't assert their own excellence by citing turgid case studies but tell stories instead, confident enough to leave readers to infer from them what they will.

It is beyond the scope of this chapter to explore every avenue of story within the world of work; and it is anyway dangerous, if tempting, to believe that story is the panacea for all corporate ills. But, as we forever emphasise on Dark Angels courses, there is one type of story that every organisation can, and should from time to time, turn to: its own founding story. The Nigerian novelist Ben Okri says, 'Stories are the secret reservoirs of value: change the stories individuals and nations live by and tell themselves and you change the individuals and nations.' The same is true for organisations. A founding story is very often the touchstone for what an organisation stands for.

A client of mine, now sadly departed, ran a successful video production and events management company. Jim Adamson was a larger-than-life character who had overcome enormous personal challenges to achieve his success. Not only had he left school at fifteen, he was also a paraplegic, paralysed in a shooting accident when he was only seventeen. Eschewing more obviously commercial locations, he ran his business, Speakeasy Productions, from a large house in a Perthshire village. Clients loved coming to visit. Jim in his wheelchair, the paterfamilias, was always there, ready to dispense bonhomie and hospitality. But few knew why he was disabled – he was not given to elaborating, and most were too polite to ask.

We discussed his story together. The more I learned of it the more inspirational I found it. Within a couple of years of the accident he was fronting a rock-and-roll band in his wheelchair. Later he enrolled for a degree in film-making at university and discovered that, despite his physical limitations, he was very good at it. One thing led to another and within a couple of decades he had built up a thriving business in what was a very competitive field. But natural modesty left him resistant to the idea of using his personal story in connection with the company. We continued the conversation, and eventually he agreed to allow his sales team to use a little of it in their presentation to a supermarket chain. Despite being the outside contender, they won the pitch. The client later confided that it was Jim's story and what it said about the company's values that had swung it for them.

In the case of the outdoor-wear company Patagonia, the name itself conjures a powerful story – of jagged mountains and glaciers, turbulent seas, wind-blasted grasslands and herds of wild vicuña. (Contrast that, for example, with Accenture, surely one of the most pointless and risible names in corporate history.)

Patagonia's backstory has even more to say about the company than its name. The founder, Yvon Chouinard, began climbing in California aged fourteen as a member of a falconry club. By the time he was eighteen he had noticed that climbing routes were strewn with soft-iron pitons which, once placed in the rock, could not be removed. He bought a forge, taught himself blacksmithing and began to make removable steel pitons. For several years he supported himself by selling the pitons out of the back of his car as he toured the US West Coast, alternately surfing and exploring new climbing routes. A free spirit, he lived hand to mouth and steeped himself in the writings of Muir, Thoreau, Emerson and Saint-Exupéry.

In time he went into partnership with an aeronautical engineer, Tom Frost. They refined the pitons and other products, and by 1970 Chouinard Equipment had become the largest supplier of climbing hardware in the US. But the steel pitons, although removable, scarred the rock, and Chouinard and Frost were purists: climbing, they believed, should be clean, leaving as little trace of the climber's ascent as possible. So, at considerable commercial risk, they launched an alternative product, an aluminium chock that could be wedged into cracks, and removed, by hand.

The risk paid off. The company prospered and in due course added a range of outdoor wear with a new brand name, Patagonia, to preserve the integrity of the original hardware brand. From the start, Patagonia's commitment to sustainability was as strong as that of its sister company. All staff are actively involved in day-to-day support for environmental causes, while a percentage of annual sales goes to grassroots environmental groups around the world. At the time of writing, November 2018, the company had recently announced that it would donate $10 million – the exact amount received as a result of what Patagonia's CEO described as the Trump administration's 'irresponsible' 2017 tax cuts – to raise awareness of climate change.

Patagonia's story is one that demonstrates real congruence between the founding spirit of the business and its behaviour today. Most people who buy its products know this.

The words of John Steinbeck, with which this chapter opens, have particular resonance in today's world of so-called fake news, fabricated stories and misinformation. Honest writing fosters understanding, he avers, which leads to kindness and love. Yet we are drowning daily in dishonest writing that fosters division and leads to hatred.

The stories I have told to illustrate this chapter represent honest writing of the kind we constantly advocate on Dark Angels courses, and therefore in each case some small advance in human understanding. There is something to learn from every story told with good intent, and it is the greatest stories that have the most to tell us.

Some years ago I contributed a chapter to a book entitled *The Bard & Co.* A 26 project, it was an exploration of what Shakespeare's plays might have to say about the modern business world. I was assigned *Romeo and Juliet*. At the time I happened to be working with the internal communications team of the drinks company Scottish & Newcastle. I proposed to them that they help me, and they agreed.

I gave each team member a character and sent them off to read the play. We then discussed it before travelling from Edinburgh to Stratford-upon-Avon for a performance by the Royal Shakespeare Company (these were pre-austerity days). Finally, each wrote a piece about the twenty-first-century drinks industry as seen from the perspective of their Shakespearean character. The results were illuminating.

Romeo and Juliet, it transpired, was not merely a love story but a tale of dithering leaders, headstrong youngsters and self-serving middle-rankers – culminating in a catastrophic, indeed fatal, failure of communication. Trust, loyalty, responsibility, moderation, foresight, co-operation, decisiveness, good leadership – or their opposites (in fact, mostly their opposites)

– were all there to be seen in the behaviour of the Montagues and the Capulets.

For the purposes of our exercise, Romeo homed in on the importance of market knowledge and branding, positioning himself as a new low-alcohol spritzer 'of complex character' for eighteen-to-thirty-year-old women. Juliet imagined herself as an ingénue, the newcomer to the sales department, who put her trust in the wrong person with disastrous consequences for the business. Mercutio, Romeo's exuberant friend and the murderous Tybalt's victim, poignantly described the betrayal felt by a long-serving employee when a part of the business was sold off. The Nurse reflected on the fact that gossip is an inescapable part of life in large organisations. The Friar wrote about the virtues of perseverance and the ubiquity of incompetence and over-promotion in FTSE 100 companies.

This greatest of all love stories contained more insight into the contemporary business world, more understanding, than I or my cast of corporate communicators could possibly have imagined.

In *Cave of Forgotten Dreams*, Werner Herzog talks to a young French scientist who spent five days in the Chauvet Cave studying the paintings and afterwards found himself dreaming constantly of lions. Was he afraid? Herzog asks. 'I was not afraid,' answers the young man in his halting English. 'No, no… it was more a feeling of powerful things and deep things, a way to understand things which is not a direct way.'

Understanding is what stories offer, a route to greater insight into ourselves and others and the world around us, a route ultimately to connection; not in a direct, didactic way but indirectly, subtly, with soft steps, through the kinds of dream or mist that storytelling conjures. That is stories' great power and their great beauty. It has been so ever since men and women first settled around the fires in their caves. And it will be when we, their twenty-first-century descendants, are nothing more than the ghosts of footsteps, no longer even faint traces in the dust.

Try this

The best and most familiar story you have to tell is your own. Take whatever time you need to write the opening paragraphs of your autobiography. You might even choose to see it as the founding story of your personal brand. Where do you start? How do you make it compelling, drawing the reader in to what you have to say? Do you recognise the voice as being distinctly your own? Do you have a title? And what *else* are you saying; what's the subtext?

3

When I was seventeen, I wrote a piece of creative non-fiction for my English A-Level. It was about my first leg-waxing experience at the age of twelve. It was funny and messy and nuanced and ridiculous and culturally specific to my experience as a hairy Indian teenage girl. But my teacher told me it couldn't work. So I wrote a piece with a white, male, blue-eyed protagonist and got an A. This is a perfect example of how, institutionally and culturally, women of colour like me are told from a very young age that our stories and experiences are not relevant enough. That certain perspectives will always be prioritised over our own. It happens in the mainstream media. In politics. In history. My identity is reduced to stereotypes and tropes. It's taken me a while to realise this, but I write because I refuse to exist in the margins. It's grounded in an instinct for survival. Every day I have to remind myself that my perspective is relevant; it's what sets me apart and gives me a competitive edge in the working world, too. I'm proud of that, and hope it empowers others to feel confident enough to tell their stories, even when those in positions of power refuse to believe in them.

Roshni Goyate, freelance senior copywriter, founder of The Other Box

SHOE BE DO: ON EMPATHY

STUART DELVES

Writing for business, one is right in the hurly-burly: the human cauldron where each of us connects with the wider world. What better place for the colour and vigour of language than the cut and thrust of commerce? For me the key to writing for business is empathy.

Early in my copywriting career I had an old pair of scuffed, cracked white shoes. I was down at heel and looking to get into a Bristol advertising agency. I had done my apprenticeship at CDP, the 'University of Advertising' and the progenitor of such classics as Benson & Hedges Gold, Parker Pens and Happiness is a Cigar Called Hamlet. I had picked up from the agency folklore that once upon a time a young art director and copywriter had pitched up for a job interview but were told 'we like your book but we're looking for an older, more experienced team'. A few days later the creative director went in to interview the next contenders on the list, only to be confronted by the young pair again; but it took a minute to recognise them, what with their ivory canes, grey wigs and deftly applied wrinkles. They got the job! Those were the days.

By 1986 I'd missed advertising's golden era of the 1960s and 1970s, but those were still the days before hideous online application forms; a good burgeoning portfolio was a better passport to the next job than a CV or an MA (Oxon). They were still the days, too, when you could chance your arm and take a gamble. Inspired by my CDP predecessors, the pretend-old geezers, I put my pitiful loafers in a cardboard shoebox and delivered the package by hand to the agency, just off Park Street. It was addressed to Steve Hall, creative director at JPH, a thrusting young 'shop' doing some exciting work – especially for the provinces, where my new wife and I had headed for the closer proximity to country pastures and a better quality of life.

On the lid of the box I wrote in block capitals: 'To respond to people's needs you have to put yourself in their shoes.' Inside, of course, were the Trojan brogues. On the side of one I wrote, again in block capitals: 'Try mine.'

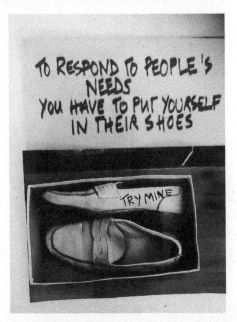

I got a letter back from Steve. He liked the shoes. He added the inevitable quip, which I suppose he couldn't resist: 'They smell.' It got me an interview. And although it didn't get me the job, here I am, thirty-two years later, still plying my trade, and I've just received an email from my Dark Angels colleague Elen Lewis with the subject title 'Glorious shoes'. She's been out to buy some postcards featuring a whole range of – as she says – 'glorious shoes', which we are going to use in an empathy exercise with a global pharmaceutical client in workshops in Boston and, via video conference, in Tokyo. One of the things we'll be keen to get across to the communications team in this 'patient-centred' company is that we're all patients: we all get sick, we all have varying levels of physical and mental health.

I suppose the shoe analogy hasn't worn thin for me over the years.

Last year, when working on a tone of voice development project for a large investment company shoes featured again, because empathy featured again, especially in the nitty-gritty echelons of answering death claims and complaints letters.

As we emphasise on Dark Angels courses, writers have two key resources: memory (experience) and imagination. Imagination often fills in the gaps, or embellishes, where memory proves fallible. Memory, really remembering what it was like – the feeling, say, of first falling in love or first having your heart broken – is vital for empathising across the generations. Too often, I find – especially with respect to young love – that people of my vintage tend to forget and minimise the depth and gravity of feelings of our real-life Romeos and Juliets, even though they're drawn again and again to the story's dramatisation on screen and stage.

The CDP team were wise enough not to feature such angst in their Hamlet ads. The situations depicted for lighting up the Happiness cigar were more humorous, like Gregor Fisher in the photo booth struggling with his hair strands, or Ian Botham the morning after he was fined £100 for being found in possession of cannabis. They pitched the empathy just right, the latter being a brilliant scoop.

In the investment company's tone of voice guide we suggested that, when writing, you should imagine what it's like to be, say, a ballerina or a spaceman, or remember what it was like playing your first game of football or getting married – in other words, putting yourself in someone else's shoes or indeed your own, younger pair of shoes. We emphasised the precious nature of the customer or client relationship, without which any service industry wouldn't exist. And, when something is precious, we handle it with care. So, handling client relationships with care is as important as handling clients' money with care.

It's important to always remember that you are a customer or client too. Remember that, when writing on behalf of a business or a brand. Think of all the irritation you've felt at being spoken to as if you were an idiot or, on the other hand, as if you should understand all the dense abstraction or technical jargon. Speaking as one human being to another, naturally, is the key to writing empathetically in business.

The financial wizard and economic commentator, Warren Buffett, once gave a great tip on this. Asked if he had someone in mind when he wrote his annual reports for Berkshire Hathaway Investments he said, 'Yes, my sisters, Doris and Bertie. They're both highly intelligent women. I love them and I respect them.' He went on to say that even though they were highly intelligent, he was aware that they didn't have his niche knowledge and understanding of financial investments, so he pitched his narrative accordingly and with the requisite warmth when talking to people he was fond of. And with a flourish of generosity, he finished off by saying, 'And if you don't have a Doris or a Bertie you can borrow mine.'

Maybe one of the clearest ways to reveal what empathy is all about is with an example of a complete lack of it. During a workshop with marketing folks from an Edinburgh pensions provider I came across a letter so startlingly lacking in empathy that I had a moment of inner apoplexy.

I had asked participants to bring along examples of both good and bad writing from the company. This is an exercise we always do on our foundation courses and it invariably leads to animated, sometimes heated, discussion. One young woman had a letter in her hand that she rightly thought was an example of bad writing. In the huge corpus of post-sales, operational 'literature' that any such organisation has, this letter had a name: the 'Existence Check' letter. This is the gist.

Granted, this is not an easy letter to write. Nevertheless, it rather cack-handedly explained that the recipient, having reached the age of seventy-five, was required by law to verify that they were still alive and therefore entitled to keep receiving their annuity. It addressed the recipient as a 'life', then went on to list who could witness their signature. It kicked off with dignitaries like a judge, a member of parliament, a magistrate or a justice of the peace before settling on humbler pillars of society like a doctor or a lawyer.

'It's not a "life" who has received this letter,' I said. 'It's your granny. She's on her own. She's lost her husband – your granddad. She's vulnerable. How many judges does she know? How many members of parliament?' The discussion began. 'It should just be her doctor,' said one. 'Or maybe her lawyer,' said another.

Exactly. Write it sensitively – without being condescending or assuming anything – and make it easy.

Someone else commented, 'But this is a standard letter used across the industry.'

'Then what an opportunity,' I said, 'to really stand out.'

There was a rather amusing postscript to this story. One of the group recounted how an illiterate pensioner from the west of Ireland was allowed to send in a thumbprint signature to verify that he was still of this earth. As the years rolled by, some actuary began to wonder just how ancient this old cove was; he was well over a hundred. The company thought they should send someone out to kick the tyres and see for themselves. The denouement is worthy of Roald Dahl. The old man was dead and had been buried years ago, but before they lowered his body into the grave the family had sliced off the golden goose of the signature thumb and popped it in the freezer – defrosting it once a year on receipt of the aforementioned mechanical letter. They must have had a tame lawyer in their pocket. Perfection. If only they'd had the sense to know when to stop.

Writing with empathy is not necessarily easy. Writers, like anyone else, are subject to negative, alienating emotions like envy and deep-set cultural prejudices. An eye-opener for me came some years ago when working on the non-statutory guidance for the Equality Act 2010. Working closely with an equality and diversity consultant led me to see just how much prejudice and the fear of others stands in the way of employing the best person for the job – fair employment procedure being a key driver for the Act.

Research helps here. Finding out more about who you're writing on behalf of or who you're writing for really helps, as does building a profile of their character, their likes and dislikes, real or imagined, as if you're creating a character for a novel or a play.

Great writers – novelists, poets, playwrights – are often said to write with compassion, which in this context means the ability to get inside the head and soul of someone lonely or psychotic or simply entirely different. There's an old adage that says, 'Write what you know.' The thing is that with imagination, we can reach all human experience. Shakespeare didn't have to be a murderer to so fully inhabit Macbeth, and Hilary Mantel didn't have to live in the sixteenth century to write so convincingly about Thomas Cromwell. The other is in us, too. Try their shoes for size.

Try this

Pick a pair of shoes – not a pair you would wear. You might see them in a shop window, in a painting, or on someone's feet. Imagine the person who wears them. Write a cameo about that person, starting with what you take from the shoes. Start by making notes about the details of the shoes: try describing them as accurately as you can. From there, proceed to imagining the person.

PART II

Developing the
Craft

4

I read the line in J. M. Coetzee's novel *Elizabeth Costello* about the core discipline of higher education being 'money-making'. I felt saddened and angry, not that this assertion was cynical, but because I wished it were not true. I wished that the real purpose of universities could shine through.

Our universities are such a vital force – for the people they reach, and for those they might. Working with institutions to help them look at the language they use in a different light, to help them tell their stories and find their voices, feels like a sacred privilege.

Paul Gentle, academic director, Invisible Grail Limited

TELL ALL THE TRUTH, BUT TELL IT SLANT

HOW EMILY DICKINSON HELPED ME BECOME A BETTER GHOSTWRITER

ELEN LEWIS

The life of a ghostwriter happens in the margins of a page. It's a shadowy world where discretion, holding secrets and keeping quiet are the tools of the trade. You need an ear for translation, an eye for a buried story, a chameleon skin that changes hue with each project and the inner confidence to understand that the book, the writing does not belong to you.

Many of us are ghostwriters without knowing it. That speech or presentation you wrote for your boss. That report you slaved over that omitted your name. The email you edited, the article you drafted, the press quote you wove out of thin air. Like many of you, I've done all of this secret writing under the cover of darkness and out it goes into the world with no connection to me.

I've ghostwritten ten published books and two nearly published books that will never hold my name on the front cover despite the fact that I crafted every single word. They are all different. They don't sound as if they share the same author, because they don't. They share the same ghostwriter and that is not the same.

Ghostwriting makes me better at the craft of writing and storytelling. There is nothing harder than writing a book for someone else. It mustn't sound like you but like the best version of your author. Here are eight rules for better writing and editing that have helped me face the blank page:

1. Tell all the truth but tell it slant.
2. It's not about you.
3. Don't tell me about birds – tell me about sparrows.
4. *Hwæt!* Never use a long word when a short word will do.
5. Ask the questions that everyone is afraid to ask.
6. All writing is rewriting.
7. Inspiration must find you working.
8. Steal like an artist.

Tell all the truth but tell it slant

Aside from the unwavering wisdom of Miss Piggy – 'Never eat more than you can lift' – I like to follow advice from nineteenth-century American poet Emily Dickinson, especially in the business of writing.

> Tell all the Truth but tell it slant –
> Success in Circuit lies
> Too bright for our infirm Delight
> The Truth's superb surprise
>
> As Lightning to the Children eased
> With explanation kind
> The Truth must dazzle gradually
> Or every man be blind –

'Tell all the truth, but tell it slant' has become a mantra, helping me write the best words with precision, meaning and soul.

First – *tell all the truth*. So much writing in business isn't truthful, and it's easy to spot. If writing is woolly and hard to understand, bloated with convoluted sentences and jargon, it's often because the writer is not telling the truth. For as Sir Peter Medawar, the Nobel Prize winner and biologist said, 'People who write obscurely are either unskilled in writing or up to mischief.'

People worry about dumbing down, that by writing something in a clear and simple way they will not be able to explain something complex. I tell them two things: first, the quote from Leonardo da Vinci, 'Simplicity is the ultimate sophistication.' Then, the fact that *The Economist* tells its journalists to ensure that every article they write, from subjects like Japanese demography to the economics of chocolate, must be understandable to a twelve-year-old child. No one will ever complain because you have made something too easy to understand.

The second nugget of advice from Emily Dickinson is probably the one that I use most in my writing and editing – *but tell it slant.*

It's about finding a new way to write something. A better angle, a better entry point. There's always a new way to write what we need to write. There's always a buried or undiscovered story.

Finding a new way to write might be technical – about setting constraints, from haikus to tricks of the alphabet and word counts. Or, finding a new way to write might come from the storytelling. I like finding parallel tales from history, science and literature that can illuminate the examples in the business books I ghostwrite. For example, in a book about big data, telling the story of Florence Nightingale's pioneering work as a data scientist was a way to 'tell all the truth but tell it slant'.

As writers we need to use the skill of empathy all the time. As ghostwriters, even more so. We need to find new ways of seeing familiar things. We need to notice hidden truths.

We run an exercise at the Dark Angels Starter Day in Strawberry Hill House, Twickenham, where writers choose an inanimate object from the eclectic gothic palace and write about it in the first person and present tense. Every piece begins, 'I AM...' These objects tell powerful stories. We hear the lamenting tales of ugly, unseen fireplaces and goldfinches trapped behind stained glass. Using the present tense makes the writing more present. Using the first person unlocks a conversational tone that's compelling and easy to read.

Charles Simic, the American poet, wrote some early poems about cutlery – a fork, a spoon, a knife. He said, 'Writers should look for what others don't see.' And 'tell it slant' is about this too.

There's always a new way to write. There's always an opportunity to tell it slant. And whether we're writing a poem, a novel, a website, copy on packaging, an annual report or someone else's speech or book – find that new angle to bring life to the writing. Because if you can make writing fizz about algorithms, you can write.

It's not about you

Many ex-journalists embark on a career of ghostwriting before realising that it's not what they hoped for. The thrill of the byline, the joy of recognition, a glimmer of fame. These things never happen for the ghostwriter. It's time to lose your ego.

It reminds me of Bette Midler's line in the film *Beaches*: 'So that's enough about me. What about you? What do you think about me?'

It's easy to fall into the trap of making the book your book, making the writing your writing. But it's not. The book does not belong to you; it belongs to your author. You can improve it and shape it and make it shine. It mustn't sound like you, but like them. Listen carefully to every word they say, understand the cadence of their conversations, the rhythm of their speech, the logic of their arguments so you can recreate it on the page

– but in a better version. Because although it must sound like they're speaking, it must be the best version of themselves. Amplified.

In time, we ghostwriters become a channel as much as a writer. We know that they would choose this word over that one, select this story over that one. Start this way, end like that.

Don't tell me about birds – tell me about sparrows

When I'm running poetry workshops for kids, I talk a lot about being specific with the words we choose. Don't tell me about birds, tell me about sparrows. Don't tell me about sweets, tell me about lemon sherbets.

Powerful writing doesn't fall into the murky waters of vague generalisations. Be specific in your examples, your opinions, your stories. Add detail.

For in the beginning was the word. Before you can write a sentence you have a word. Increase your word power. Words are the raw material of our craft. Challenge every word, for the words we use are the worlds we live in. Expand your vocabulary. Bring a dull piece of writing to life.

Listen to the word out loud. Indian words like *pyjamas* and *bungalow* have a soft bumbling bounce about them. My favourite word is *hiraeth*. It's a Welsh word without a direct translation. It's tinged with sadness and means a longing, a yearning, a homesickness for what once was.

What's your favourite word?

Words can do everything. They can inspire tears, laughter and revolution. They can change hearts and minds. They can influence, illuminate, challenge. They can persuade people to do what you want. They can help someone fall in love with you. Poet Simon Armitage writes, 'In choosing a word, you're making a statement.' So choose carefully, choose well.

Hwæt! Never use a long word when a short word will do

We can all learn from the Anglo-Saxons, who would begin each important speech with *Hwæt!*

There was an Anglo-Saxon word *ban-hus*. It meant bonehouse and was used to describe the human body. It is a word painting. Anglo-Saxon poets used word paintings to vary their descriptions of long journeys and epic battles. In *Beowulf*, the epic Anglo-Saxon poem, the sea is a whale-road, ligaments are bone-locks, the sun is a sky-candle and icicles are water-ropes.

English is better than Latin. You don't exterminate, you kill. You don't salivate, you drool. You don't conflagrate, you burn.

For as Tim Radford, former *Guardian* science editor, wrote in his twenty-five commandments for journalists:

> Moses did not say to Pharaoh: 'The consequence of non-release of one particular subject ethnic population could result ultimately in some kind of algal manifestation in the main river basin, with unforeseen outcomes for flora and fauna, not excluding consumer services.'
>
> He said, 'The waters which are in the river ... shall be turned to blood, and the fish that is in the river shall die, and the river shall stink.'[1]

Choose Anglo-Saxon words over French or Latin words. Never use a long word when a short word will do. But always be prepared to ignore the rules when you need an exact word that is otherwise not available.

---

1. 'A manifesto for the simple scribe – my 25 commandments for journalists' by Tim Radford, Wednesday 19 January 2011, *The Guardian*.

Ask the questions that everyone is afraid to ask

When I'm at the beginning of a ghostwriting project, I feel like a moth drawn to the lamp in the corner of the room, bumping into things, looking for the light, grasping for meaning.

The ghostwriter comes to a new subject with a clear head and a blank page. While an author may have grappled with a complex issue for decades before deciding to capture the idea in a book, the ghostwriter must become a translator within weeks. It's a privilege to absorb and then communicate the thoughts of experts. But it's a steep, steep learning curve. Instead of feeling intimidated, embrace the value of not understanding everything. Ask the questions everyone is afraid to ask. They don't make you look stupid, they make you look smart.

All writing is rewriting

Truman Capote wrote, 'I believe more in the scissors than I do in the pencil.' Brilliant writers tend to be brilliant editors. Or they're lucky enough to have one. Advertising guru David Ogilvy knew a thing or two about good writing. He said, 'I'm a lousy copywriter but I am a good editor. So I go to work editing my own draft. After four or five editings, it looks good enough to show to the client.'

Here are some tricks for editing:

Give yourself some space between writing and editing. Take your time. Don't edit on screen; print it out. Read the words aloud, listen to the rhythm. If you run out of breath, your sentences are too long. If your mind wanders, you're boring yourself...

On Writing

What you leave out is as important as what you put in. Create that space, those silences. As readers, sometimes we need to breathe, and sometimes we need to run. It's like composing a piece of music.

Sometimes you have to start all over again and again and again until you write it right. It was Roald Dahl who said that all writing is rewriting. In a letter to his daughter, Lucy, he talked about his experience of writing *Matilda*:

> The reason I haven't written you for a long time is that I have been giving every moment to getting a new children's book finished. And now at last I have finished it, and I know jolly well that I am going to have to spend the next three months rewriting the second half. The first half is great, about a small girl who can move things with her eyes and about a terrible headmistress who lifts small children up by their hair and hangs them out of upstairs windows by one ear. But I've got now to think of a really decent second half. The present one will all be scrapped. Three months work gone out the window, but that's the way it is. I must have rewritten Charlie [and the Chocolate Factory] five or six times all through and no one knows it.

In the same way, Matisse worked on his painting *Bathers by a River* for eight years between 1909 and 1917 until he was happy with it. In 2010, MoMA curators used X-ray technology to reveal how much he painted and repainted the canvas. On video you can see how dramatically and obsessively the piece was reworked. So rewrite, rewrite and then rewrite again. But know that you will have to stop – we all have deadlines to meet.

Inspiration must find you working

Pablo Picasso said, 'Inspiration exists but it must find you working.' For there is no substitute for the graft of the thing. The turning up. The sitting at the desk. The writing of the words, one after the other until you reach the end. The ability to keep writing, whether you're in the mood or not. That's all. And sometimes the muse will come, and sometimes she won't. 'Show up, show up, show up,' said novelist Isabel Allende.

Steal like an artist

We learn by copying. When my son Arthur was three years old he pretended he could read by memorising favourite books like a party trick. But then suddenly he crossed the line and he could read. Imitate writers you admire.

Hunter S. Thompson copied *The Great Gatsby* and *A Farewell to Arms* on a typewriter while he was working at *Time* magazine. He wanted to understand how F. Scott Fitzgerald and Ernest Hemingway constructed sentences, chose words. He wanted to get inside their heads, under their skin, into their pen.

All reading is rereading. There's power in a close examination of the text. It's like watching someone dance and then secretly in your own room trying to work out the steps. It's about taking the craft seriously and doing everything you can to improve.

Here's something we can all do as writers. Take a favourite book and handwrite a passage you love. Notice everything. The punctuation, sentences, the way it sounds in your head, the words they choose, the rhythm of the lines. The spaces and pauses.

T. S. Eliot, one of my favourite poets, wrote, 'Immature poets imitate, mature poets steal.' So here's a poem I wrote, stealing inspiration from his poem *Portrait of a Lady*. First I copied it. Then I took the mood, the image and created an imaginative space of my own.

Still August afternoon
Sky presses down
Ants with sticky wings
Crowd airwaves,
Bump into things.

The garden roses bloom
Then die in this stifling room.
Curtains glow, Chopin soars in,
Out. You sigh,
'I'm losing my mind.'

It begins. I do not know
I mean to say,
I cannot know,
Would like to know
What this all means.

Rewriting, ghostwriting. It's still writing. It's still the craft of choosing the best words and putting them in the best order. The understanding that meaning happens in between, on the blank spaces on a page. Knowing that words can soar and plummet, shine and soften, shriek and whisper. Feeling in your heart that the words you write can change the person you are and touch the people who read them. That the writing of the writing, whether it's for someone else or just for you, whether it's for a floodlit stage or a dark corner, that the writing of the writing is a noble and worthwhile craft, and all we can do is keep writing the writing, rewriting the writing, rewriting the writing, until we've crafted something of slantish truth and beauty.

Exercise one on the power of imitation

Read the poem 'This Is Just To Say' by William Carlos Williams, where he writes about eating all the plums in the icebox. It is written as though it were a note left on the kitchen table. Something found. It begins, *This is just to say*, with the final stanza beginning, *Forgive me.*

Use the existing simple structure of the poem as a stepping stone. Keep as many key lines as you wish but certainly – *This is just to say, I have…* and *Forgive me…* and write a response.

Here's one I prepared earlier…

This is just to say
I have swallowed
Your silence
That was on
The table

And which
You were probably
Saving
Forever

Forgive me
It was delightful
So sharp
And so cold.

Try this as a daily practice with other poems (e.g. 'The Red Wheelbarrow' by William Carlos Williams) and other poets.

Try this

Exercise two on the power of imitation

You will need a newspaper article or the page from an old book that you don't mind marking, and a black marker pen. This exercise is inspired by a British artist called Tom Phillips who creates works of art from second-hand books by drawing around them and blacking out words to create poetry. He calls these poems *A Humument*. One line might read, 'wanted. a little white opening out of thought'.

Take a newspaper article and a black marker pen. Circle random words of meaning. Black out the words you don't want. Keep working until some lines of poetry emerge. It's not copying. It's creating.

Think how you might use these techniques in other forms of writing. Yes, even in that company policy document on sustainability.

5

I often say that I am a researcher by training and a writer at heart. Colleagues have told me this strapline undersells my twenty-five-year career working on brands. Yet, those two career passions – research and writing – are the foundation of what I do and why I do it. Research fuels my curiosity. Writing lets me do something with it.

Early in my business career, I noticed that people divided writing into two camps – business writing and creative writing. I wholeheartedly rejected this notion. Any opportunity to write was an opportunity to create. I believe you have to do what you love as much as you love what you do. And I loved writing. I could not imagine a work life in business without writing words that let me be creative. More importantly, I only wanted to write words that people would enjoy reading.

Laurence Vincent is the chief brand officer of UTA in California and the author of Brand Real *and* Legendary Brands

DESIGNING THOUGHTS ON A PAGE

GILLIAN COLHOUN

Perfection is boring. Getting better is where all the fun is.

So let's get better. But let's have fun too.

As creative professionals, we mostly live within the fine print of our labels: writer, designer, film-maker, illustrator, photographer. But if we only do those things, we're missing out on a huge opportunity for growth. We should explore the full range of our creative selves.

Creativity is an elusive thing: it's personal and often unconscious. As Ray Kroc put it, 'Creativity is a highfalutin word for the work I have to do between now and Tuesday.' Still, writers are creators and we benefit from knowing how to manage that process, no matter how chaotic it may feel at the time.

For twenty years, I've written in the company of designers. I noticed early on that, while the outcomes of their work change massively, their methods and mindset follow a systematic pattern – a pattern they articulate, use and in some cases trademark. I also speak to ridiculously talented writers who, after completing a sizeable project, say, 'I'd never do it that way again.'

There are countless books extolling the wisdom designers can learn from writers. Rightly so; writing is important to design. This chapter isn't about that, nor is it about pretending there's a secret sauce or rigid formula. It's about being open to a different perspective; observing the ways we, as writers, can adapt from the world of design to make our methods more harmonious and our thinking more original. After all, design is good at two things all great writing needs – insight and empathy.

Everything seems impossible until it's done

It's seductive to think that people who make physical artefacts, like engineers and architects, have it easy. They have a three-dimensional thing to build, to make appear within a clear process. But are writers so very different?

Fun etymology fact: the word poetry comes from the Greek *poiein*, 'to make'. A poem is made. It is the poet then who creates a notion that is unmistakably a thing, a noun. As Shakespeare writes in *A Midsummer Night's Dream*:

> The poet's eye, in a fine frenzy rolling,
> Doth glance from heaven to earth, from earth to heaven;
> And as imagination bodies forth
> The forms of things unknown, the poet's pen
> Turns them to shapes, and gives to airy nothing
> A local habitation and a name.

Writing, just like design, is a process as well as an outcome. Far from being linear, it's a swirling mass of looping back to different stages. It's messy, often perplexing, but it can be joyous too. Design thinking is an approach that gives people like you and me a way to solve the unsolvable. Or to put it another way, a way to feel more confident about leaping into the complexity of bringing something useful or beautiful or poetic into the world.

It's thought that counts

Let's start with two mindsets that are not only central to all design practice, but to all Dark Angels courses.

Give yourself permission to think differently.

I like to think of this as creative cross-training. For a writer, that could mean starting a project with a drawing instead of words. It could mean picking up a camera instead of a pen; or opening up a conversation instead of a laptop. This initial approach can at first feel strange or messy (which I like), but this unstructured work practice encourages new muscles to develop and captivating ideas to germinate.

Throw off your ego and adopt the beginner's attitude

Assume nothing. A concept from Zen Buddhism called shoshin, the 'beginner's mind', is a way to throw off preconceptions and adopt an attitude of openness. As the monk Shunryu Suzuki says, 'In the beginner's mind there are many possibilities, but in the expert's mind there are few.' Designers know the value of approaching subjects as a novice. Even if you already know a lot, it makes you more willing to experiment, to ask why and question the status quo. Questions are important. Why is that?

No one starts from nowhere

Where you begin influences where you go next. Every designer of every denomination begins with a brief. Designing a building, or a typeface, can be a long journey, so it's wise to have a clear vision of its purpose. But isn't that just as true of a novel, a poem or the FAQs on a website?

The key will always be in understanding the nature of that purpose; taking an elevated view to stop, pause, wait, consider the big picture. Since writers are often intellectually and physically separated from the tribe, we're often at war with ourselves. Where to start? What the hell am I doing? Why did I say yes to this? When will it end? These existential acts of decision-making are largely subjective. Without context or challenge, we can become lazy and do too little, or worse, too much.

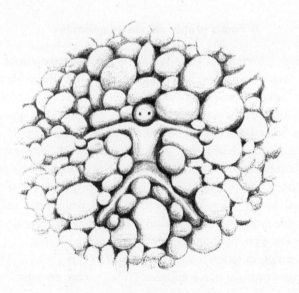

Design thinking is a way to circumvent the mousetraps. Here's a quick rationale from Tom Kelley of IDEO, the Californian design consultancy:

> Before you had design thinking and somebody gave you a big problem, a very difficult problem, you'd say, 'I have no idea how I'm going to do that, I'm going to have to hope that I have a big idea.' You'd say, 'I'm smart, I hope I have a big idea.' You'd think of it as a personal goal. Once you have design thinking in your life, you get to the point where, when somebody gives you a big problem, you have creative confidence. You say, 'I know how to do this. I'll collaborate. I'll build prototypes. I'll understand the users to get the ideas for what is really meaningful to the people that I'm designing for. I'll bet you I come up with something with purpose, with intention, something that's successful.' That's confidence.

Confidence to stretch past the fear and the banal? Yes, please.

Smart people ask stupid questions

Happily, this is a really big deal at my kids' primary school. No one asks more questions than a four-year-old. But there's an art to asking that goes beyond clarification. How to frame a question is at the root of everything a designer (and a writer) does. In today's 'always on' world, there's a rush to answer, not ask. And I like that asking requires both vulnerability and confidence. Today, when invited or compelled to write anything, my first response is to ask why. It can take several 'whys' to get there, but that short word will always elicit a valuable conversation, even an internal one, to reveal truth over assumption, no matter what I'm writing.

A simple question to ask yourself is, 'How might I...?' These simple words are transformative. Now you are presented with an opportunity, not a problem – an optimistic invitation to experiment and explore. A solid 'How might I' question has a nifty way of permitting broad brushes with enough focus to give you a place to start.

Eyes wide open

Designers are natural magpies. They listen with their eyes as well as their ears. They understand that everything has the potential to inspire. They take pictures, make voice memos, collect images, build libraries of small but significant moments and images. Sound familiar? So many writers begin a story because they have an image in their mind that they just can't shake off until they've written about it.

Short story writer Claire Keegan told me once that, 'Readers will follow your pictures as long as you provide them. Give them the time, place and person so they know who and what to follow.'

Science tells me that imagination is dependent on observation. If we want to use our imagination in our writing, we need first to develop our ability to look. Designers are trained to understand human behaviours so they can empathise with the people they are designing for. In other words, to grasp insights that reveal new and unexplored ways of seeing, they have a deep human focus.

For the writer, the desires of our readers and our characters emerge from what we know, feel and see. We use senses to guide the narrative through an incision in time or the subject at hand. Looking through the eyes of one person, the reader understands everything she is experiencing. Whether that's developing character in a story or creating audience personas for a website, the ability to look and see will spark fresh thinking.

You can't wait for inspiration; go after it

When it comes to idea generation, design requires both broad and exploratory methods (divergent thinking) as well as prioritisation and focus (convergent thinking). Pairing the two approaches increases the chances of finding the most effective answers to often difficult challenges.

When nothing is certain, everything is possible.

Divergent thinking explores many possibilities, defers judgement and creates an open space to nurture the maximum number of ideas and points of view. In other words, it permits thinking without restraint. Many of us have experienced the brainstorming meeting where an enthusiastic facilitator tells us there's no such thing as a bad idea. And yes, the collective sigh can be palpable.

But divergent thinking is more than just brainstorming. It's taking a challenge and attempting to identify all the possible factors, then listing all the ways they can be addressed. In writing, we'd call this automatic writing where, with a simple prompt, we get down on paper whatever comes to mind without stopping to proofread or edit. This can help generate a variety of thoughts in a short period of time for review later.

Piggybacking on one idea to stimulate others is another divergent thinking technique. A mash-up approach can be a thrilling way to pose bold, even unreasonable questions to speed along our thinking. For example, when designers are tasked with making school lunches healthy, they might ask, 'What is the farmer's market version of a school canteen?' Or if they're developing a money management app for teenagers, they'd consider, 'What's the WhatsApp version of a savings account?' The trick is to layer a real-world example of whatever quality you seek onto what you're designing.

In writing, I use this technique all the time, particularly when it comes to defining and applying tone of voice. If a brand should sound authoritative, I'll ask myself, 'How might *West Wing* President Jed Bartlet deliver this message?' If playful was the high note, then how might David Sedaris phrase it?

Another useful variation of the design mash-up is to ask, 'What if?' What if this character were not so confident? What if the hero were ugly instead of handsome? What if the girl refused the handsome prince?

These types of divergent techniques deliberately ignore the constraints of reality to push past the obvious and explore new ground. The experience puts our writing in different places, giving our reader and characters new frames of reference. More importantly, they make new connections.

A fashion designer will spend hours playing with fabric, arranging it one way, then another and then another, trying different configurations to see how they work. It looks a lot like playing, because it's fun to do. It's the same with writing. If I enjoy it, I'll do more of it.

At Dark Angels, we actively encourage creative playfulness and it's why we try to make every course a place to play, yes, but also to discover, fail and try out new ideas. Like the fashion designer and her materials, it's exhilarating to arrange and rearrange words, invent new thoughts, rhythms and images.

Only when you are organised can you truly be free

Of course, at some point decisions need to be made. Which ideas are worthy of prototyping, building or testing? The convergent stage of the process is one of refinement and synthesis, taking an idea from a world where anything is possible to a point where only limited options are viable.

Convergence is about introducing the restraints of context to your best thoughts – extracting real value out of novel ideas and exposing them to the real world. One way to do this is to select a pattern of organisation by grouping similar things together. Give each group a name. What stands out about the different categories? Try sketching a diagram or ask yourself for a two-second instinctive reaction. Make lots of prototypes and test them on critical friends. Or talk through your thoughts to someone who's not involved in the project. Once a challenge is described in sufficient detail, there's something truly magical about stating your thinking aloud in such a way that the answer appears in all its obvious glory.

There are lots of examples of convergent thinking that demonstrate the necessity for this kind of technique. In the film *Apollo 13*, the astronauts are trying to generate enough power to get the capsule back to Earth. The chief orders his team to make the capsule simulator 'cold and dark' and create 'the exact same conditions they've got'. When one of his engineers announces, 'I need a flashlight,' the response is, 'That's not what they have up there. Don't give them anything they don't have on board.' The harsh reality of the constraint elicited a demanding but more valuable solution.

Learn from failure early

I'm often asked by other business writers how to avoid endless rewrites. With client work, this has rarely been a problem; not because I hit it out of the park every time, but because I'm happy to pull back the curtain and invite those same clients into the process. Designers call this co-creation. I simply call it working on the same team. The divergent element of this stage usually takes the form of a workshop where the room is covered in prompts, scribbles, insights and images. It's chaos.

Then I take it all away. My role is to apply the convergent thinking – connecting patterns, grouping categories, pinpointing outliers, compounding the fragments and nailing the abstract. This design-led path allows me to create a prototype, or in writers' lexicon, the first draft.

Prototypes are useful because they help designers learn from failure early and inexpensively. Most importantly, they invite others to react to an idea. A prototype is also a concept most business clients understand. When they view your work through the lens of a contextualised and considered process, they respect it. They respect you. And that makes the notion of testing those models (think landing pages on a website, or clicks on a call to action) a way of validating and improving, not hindering, your efforts.

Drawing is another way to make prototyping work hard for the writer. Sketching is a skill I'm working on. I'm not much of an artist but that's OK. I adopted the beginner's mindset, bought a book, enrolled at a class and I've since graduated from sketching umbrellas and speech bubbles to drawing actual people doing things like riding a bike or eating a sandwich.

Why? The media I write for are continually changing. When I'm writing scripts for animations and films, the storyboarding process is so much more joyful (and efficient) when I collaborate with the animator on both visual and verbal planes. On a recent project for the BBC, I worked with an indie studio to develop scripts for ten GCSE Bitesize learning videos. The first drafts came back from the commissioning editor with minimal changes – a first for the film studio, and a ringing endorsement for writers who think visually.

Let the cave dweller roar

Telling stories through structure, tension, tone and perspective feels natural and intuitive. We all know the power behind the skills of the storyteller. But if telling stories is really about effective communication, there are many more tools at our disposal.

I know this because I have a dyslexic child. She is smart, but words can be barriers as well as doors to deeper understanding. The energy required to read (and understand) a passage about tectonic plates can be ten times that of a non-dyslexic child with a similar IQ. She is a classic visual learner. But guess what? We all are.

Designer ShaoLan Hsueh developed Chineasy, a learning method that explains thousands of Chinese characters using just a couple of hundred building blocks. By revealing the essence of something so abstract, she enabled anyone to learn it.

With client work, my visual thinking improves when I work alongside a designer right from the start. I might throw them something rough and ready (my prototype). We'll each work in turn until we have something solid, refined and considered. But in that first prototype I try hard to consider principles of layout and composition. I look at the shape of my paragraphs on the page, paying attention to proximity, white space, hierarchy and colour. Ultimately, if you present something in a dense, encyclopaedic way, it will be perceived as something dense and encyclopaedic.

Typography, too, can carry meaning through mood and tone. In Gary Hustwit's film *Helvetica*, Jonathan Hoefler talks about typefaces having their own voice. Is the type cheerful or dour, relaxed or in a hurry, serious or playful? You can even go online and match your own personality to a font. (I'm Futura, apparently.)

Just like writers, designers use metaphors all the time. Take a look at Le Corbusier's iconic LC4 chair – a cowboy lying back, feet up, smoking a pipe. Or Philippe Starck's Excalibur toilet brush: a simple everyday plastic object elevated to the status of King Arthur's mythical sword. Visual metaphors used this way are valuable, because they are eloquent. An elegant design solution is much like any other – one that meets all apparent conditions with a pleasing economy of means. To quote Claire Keegan again, 'It takes me a long time to make those stories short.' So if we can tell a story by using an image, we probably should.

Every human being is a designer

There are many definitions of what a designer does. My favourite has to be Norman Potter's, when he says a designer transforms constraint into opportunity. Isn't that what we as writers do every day? We create things with people in mind, because the more we understand about those people, the more our work will connect. In that regard, design thinking isn't just for designers. It's for everyone; but particularly we writers, who find ourselves inching our way through a dark tunnel seeing a few feet in front but having no idea where we'll end up. We are all holding candles in the dark. All we can do is keep looking and learning, creating time and space to do our best work and be ready for it when it comes along.

Try this

The only way to create an original piece of writing is to use observations unique to you. And the best way to observe is to draw. Grab a pen and a notebook; nothing fancy. Now, choose a subject to draw. This can really be anything: the dog, the person sitting opposite you, the skyline. Now, set a timer for two minutes and start drawing. Don't look at the paper while you draw. Look only at what you're drawing. When the timer goes, stop.

Like automatic writing, this is an exercise to loosen you up. But you might also notice something new about your subject – the shape, the pleasing mark-making or the way you stopped making assumptions and only drew what was there in front of you. It's a different way of seeing.

6

I write for the same reason Wile E. Coyote paints tunnels on mountainsides. I write because I get a headache when I talk. I write because I can't uproot a tree and attach it to an email and say this is what I mean. I write because of Donald Trump. I write because I need the money and I need the money to write. I write because it is a way of turning the lights on in the universe. I write because I can hardly hear myself think. I write for the reader running out the other side of the mountain.

Nick Asbury is a writer at Asbury & Asbury, author of Perpetual Disappointments Diary, *and scribbler of realtime poetry on Instagram. instagram.com/nickasbury*

I SPEAK OF THE THINGS THAT ARE THERE[1]

RICHARD PELLETIER

... if you love something enough and pay a passionate enough attention to it, the whole world can become present in it.
John Jeremiah Sullivan

What does it mean for a writer to pay attention?

Here in my writing shed, under a starry night and an almost full moon, on the southern tip of this magical island in Puget Sound where I live, I imagine rummaging through a junk drawer. Amid the rubber bands and the old paper clips, I am looking for a commemorative 1955 silver dollar that exists only in my dreams—heads on both sides. On one—the profile of the writer James Baldwin. I flip the coin. There is the curly-headed pate of my hero, the photographer Robert Frank. *My* America.

There was something on the wind in that year of 1955. Those two men, one black, one white, *knew*. Both were artists, both living in New York City. From the Village came Baldwin with *Notes of a Native Son*. 'The people who think of themselves as white,' he wrote, 'have the choice of becoming human or irrelevant. Or, as they are indeed already, in all but actual fact, obsolete.' That same year, Frank, Swiss-born, celebrated here and in Europe, set out on a series of road trips in his 1950 Ford Business Coupe (Detroit, Savannah, Miami, New Orleans, Houston, Los Angeles) to document America in a book. The time was ripe.

---

1. From Robert Frank's Guggenheim Grant application. 'I speak of the things that are there, anywhere and everywhere—easily found, not easily selected and interpreted.'

The show-stopping cover of Frank's book, *The Americans*, might well have flown straight out of James Baldwin's tightly coiled rage. Five passengers sit perfectly and eternally framed in front-to-back order on a New Orleans streetcar. A white man, a white woman. A little white boy in a little white-boy suit. (Already impressive at white entitlement.) A little white girl, crying. A black man. A black woman. In a single photograph—a supremely painful and complicated three-hundred-year story. *The Americans* was a brutally honest chronicle. *Look*, it said. Open your eyes. *Feel*. It was the book that changed photography for all time.

Miner, shaman, brother, thief

Why is this piece of writing about writing concerning itself with the double helix that is James and Robert? My brief is to talk about writing from the perspective of a photographer. And, it's because good writing always concerns itself with seeing. And seeing is what James Baldwin and Robert Frank did better than almost anyone else. Each man came to it in different ways. Baldwin's gaze was unforgiving; ethical, moral, and penetrating. Loving. It was psychological, spiritual, cultural, and personal. He was sort of an apostle of humanism. Frank's seeing was psychic surveillance. Cunning and skeptical. Exploitative. Also loving. He was a miner and a shaman, a brother and a thief. What writer wouldn't want to be all that?

There is no evidence that Baldwin and Frank knew or influenced each other. But they were working the same dark alleys—the twisted knot of American identity. 'Our dehumanization of the negro then,' wrote Baldwin, 'is indivisible from our dehumanization of ourselves. The loss of our own identity is the price we pay for our annulment of his.' I pause for a quick daydream where I see Banksy, under cover of darkness, spray-painting those words on the side of Robert Frank's New Orleans streetcar.

Frank showed us something we hadn't seen before. America as a dangerous, nervous, deeply weird, beautiful, and lonely place. Everything in conflict with everything else. Not the least of which was the story we were telling ourselves about who and what we were. (This was 1955, remember.) He tunneled down much further than was comfortable. His coda to fellow artists who might be paying attention to his work (and there were legions) was: *go deeper*. That is the single best piece of advice a writer could ever hope to hear.

I came to Baldwin much later. Born poor, black, and bisexual in Harlem, he told *Life* magazine:

> An artist is a sort of emotional or spiritual historian. His role is to make you realize the doom and glory of knowing who you are and what you are. He has to tell, because nobody else can tell, what it is like to be alive.

It's gray outside this morning—the sun is a half-lit, milky stain as it slides behind a bank of Douglas fir outside my window. I am back at it, trying to stare down this dastardly task: to say something useful about writing and photography. So it occurs to me to talk about love. To say love is at the heart of all this. First, James Baldwin and Robert Frank both have said they loved America. Their love was complicated, but they were writing and shooting from *that place*. I *loved*—and still love—those Robert Frank pictures. They changed me from the inside out. I love them madly. I have never been the same since the moment I first saw them. That body of work held me upside down and shook me until finally, I came to understand their code:

It is possible to make something beautiful and lasting and soul-shaking from the place where *you*—your heart and soul, your voice, your shame, your fear, your oddball ways—meet the world.

That changed everything. When you know something like that, down to the bone, all kinds of wonderful trouble is yours. Because now you believe. You believe in the premise at the root of all art-making. Most worrisome of all, you now believe that *you*—yes, you aspiring writer, painter, musician, sculptor, playwright—might wear the hat, too. To coin a phrase, you are fucked. Which is glorious.

A secret

All this inconveniently dovetailed with my beloved, fiercely believing mother's favorite Life Lesson: 'You can be anything you want to be, as long as you want it bad enough.' I confess that I thought I wanted to be Robert Frank. But underneath it all, chained up and locked down like Houdini, buried six feet into the bottom of a frozen lake, was my secret. I only ever wanted to be a writer. Too dangerous, so I spent years taking pictures, and I still do. But it has taken me until this moment, on this gray, overcast November morning, to unlock a mystery. Robert Frank, photographer, was my first writing teacher. His courage gave me mine.

'I worked myself into a state of grace' – Robert Frank

The lessons that Robert Frank has brought to my writing life are endless and ongoing. Pay attention. Go to those places—physical and emotional—that aren't safe or comfortable and *look*. More important, *feel*. Bring your *whole* self. Believe what you see, but stay skeptical. Get ahold of it and report back. There are stories everywhere. An empty highway at twilight. The glowing jukebox in a dive bar. An empty café with Oral Roberts on the television. The cowboy on a Manhattan street. Gas tanks, post offices, backyards. Shift the background to the foreground. Break the rules. Do it your own way. Aim higher. And higher still. Get angry. The shadows are more interesting than the light, except for the times when a crushing daylight is the story. Keep your ear to the ground. Leave some work for the viewer or the reader to do. Find new ways to tell the story. When it comes time to edit, go deeper. Find the most ruthless, merciless, and intuitive version of yourself and go to work. Robert Frank took 27,000 photographs for *The Americans*. His book has just eighty-three pictures. It was during a year-long, deliberate editing and sequencing process that the form and the idea and the *structure* became the thing that we know today. About the entire project, Robert Frank has said, 'I worked myself into a state of grace.'

'We tell ourselves stories in order to live' – Joan Didion

I was sixteen or seventeen at the time. My grandfather lived across the street from us. I would visit on a fairly regular basis—to bring over meals my mother had cooked, or just to check in. On one particular day, I gave a soft knock on his door, and let myself in. His apartment had that old-world, grandparent charm; a lot of wood and carpeting, built-in glass and wood cabinets. Dark and quiet. He was all alone those days; my grandmother had died some years before. His TV-watching chair was empty, the television was off. But he was there all right, in the room, seated at a card table. The table was crammed—set for six people. Plates, glassware, silverware, everything you'd need if everyone came to dinner. Everyone being himself, his wife, and his four children. But he was alone. Except that he wasn't, not quite. On each of five plates, he'd placed a framed photograph. I scanned the table. There was my father, my two uncles, my aunt, and my grandmother. Everyone had come to dinner. My grandfather was in conversation with all of them. He turned to me—an actor breaking the fourth wall—and whispered that they'd all come, finally, and wasn't it wonderful. He turned back to the play. He was wearing two pairs of pants—he'd nap during the day, wake up confused, and get dressed again. I willingly accepted the fiction—and the truth—of all that was in front of me. I may have become a photographer that day. Or, a storyteller. Or, a human being. Joan Didion was right: we tell ourselves stories in order to live.

A state of grace

Nothing prepared you for writing quite like being a photographer in the days of film. You'd find yourself out in the world—say, Chinatown in New York, or on the coast of California. Endless possibilities for making pictures. Your camera is loaded with Kodak Tri-X film, thirty-six frames. You're in a bit of a zone, the light is beautiful, and you're working. Two weeks later, after you've developed your fifteen rolls from that day, you have printed your contact sheets, and you find there is nothing. You have 500-plus images and not a single one is more than a humble, pleasing record or a dumb cliché. You will try to convince yourself otherwise. You will lie to yourself, possibly for weeks. Maybe this frame, maybe that one. But it's all useless, there's nothing there. There is no better training for the excruciating experience of writing first drafts.

So something happened in the relentless effort. In the absurd amount of failure. In the commitment to *trying*—and the occasional succeeding—that laid the groundwork for a step into the void. My wife and I spent the first two years of our life together on opposite coasts. We spent hours and hours on the phone. She knew me as a photographer. One night I said, 'I'm going to say something to you now, and I ask that you say absolutely nothing after I say it.' 'Okay,' she said. I said, 'I want to write.'

The sun has returned to its milky, half-hidden ways. It's cold outside. The wind is up. The stand of fir out past my window is telling its proud, steadfast, multi-generational tale. Later this afternoon, Linda and I will travel to the north end of the island to visit a sawmill. On that hour-long ride—through stands of fir and cedar and small towns, I'll be thinking about a photograph I saw the other day. It's Robert Frank, ninety-three years old, sitting out in front of his home in New York City. The backdrop is gritty. A green metal door, a brick section of wall, a green metal screen. The paint on the door frame is chipped and worn. And there he sits, a little hunched over. Still has his hair. He's an old man looking straight into the camera, a father who has outlived his two children, who both died tragically. His cane is at hand. I imagine James Baldwin sitting right next to him, the other side of the coin. If he was still here, he'd be ninety-three, too. I imagine the two of them, finally having met, after all these years of crossing paths, comparing notes. If I were there, I'd be at a loss for words. For what to say to the two storytellers who saw America, who told us everything. Who spoke of the things that were there, who told us of the doom and the glory of who we are. Who left us their songs to sing.

Try this

Get yourself a family photograph. An old photograph or a recent one will work, but it's preferable to choose one of someone close to you. Use the photograph as a springboard into a work of imagination with two threads. One thread might describe (in full Technicolor) the dreams this person had for their life. And the other thread may be what that life actually was like. Is there a way you can tie the dream and the lived life together? Are there common themes? Do the two worlds look anything alike? What feelings can you evoke in the reader about this character's dreams? And what feelings can you evoke about the real life that was lived?

84

PART III

Writing That
Works at Work

7

When growing up I was very mischievous, and I'd always tell exaggerated stories. I liked the drama. My friends' laughs, groans and 'ooh's. I've always liked concocting things that can be celebrated. I painted little models and pieced together football teams on video games. These days I follow food recipes. And I *still* tell stories.

Pair these characteristics with a childhood filled with Hogwarts magic, *Coronation Street*, a few good English teachers and encouraging parents, and this is the makings of why I'm a writer. I've learned that the world needs more of us, too. People who can craft memorable messages, share ideas and inspire others through stories and words.

Bert Preece, copywriter, winner of the first
26 Emerging Writer Award

THE SURGEON, THE ELEPHANT AND THE MAP-MAKER

AND OTHERS YOU DON'T USUALLY FIND IN A BANK

MIKE GOGAN

If you've ever had dealings with a bank, you've played your part in a story familiar to us all.

Let me tell the story through a couple I know, Liam and Rachel.

The story starts well for them...

We were renting, sharing a house with another couple. Young, happy, working hard and having fun in the soft spots between. And we were saving, too.

It was exciting to share at first. Independence, freedom, the responsibility of bill-paying. Sharing with another couple was supposed to be domestic bliss until their noise didn't match our noise, their wash ended up in our wash, their buttery knife in our pot of jam.

Time to get a place of our own. It was a commitment already written in our hearts.

We cemented that commitment into bricks and mortar one Friday evening. We were staying in; a bottle of Barbaresco; our favourite spaghetti alla puttanesca; a good movie on TV.

In an ad break a beautifully styled young couple appears. They're not unlike us. Through smiles, soft focus and slow motion they look at a *For Sale* sign on a desirable property that has magically built itself into reality off a set of plans. A wistful, loving gaze sparks between them as they recognise their dream coming true.

'Make it home' is the encouraging end line from a bank.

Watching this, we decide it's time for action.

The following Monday at lunchtime we walk into a branch of the same bank. We meet Kate. Her handshake and eye contact tell us she's trained well and knows her stuff.

Half an hour later, Kate shows us out and we're clutching a letter telling us how much we can confidently borrow in principle. There's hundreds of thousands burning in our hands, and its warmth shows in the tone of the letter. Of course there are conditions, but we're glowing in the mutual trust shared with the Bank of Kate; we can go house-hunting.

A few weeks later and we've found a place of our own. A little shabby, but we're the type of people who like to put our mark on a home. Kate says we're approved for enough to pay for the house and for our refurb.

We've been trading paperwork with Kate through a handy app on our phones – a shot of our passports is enough to identify us; a valuation is quick and easy. Kate ticks the boxes while we're fine-tuning plans for paintwork.

The Bank of Kate is good and we're all systems go – good to go. We're excited and happy. We always knew it was a big move, and it's about to get quite serious. Kate presses a button that makes money flow to our lawyer. It seems that button has 'IT'S TIME TO GET VERY SERIOUS' written on it, because what happens next is that everything falls off the edge of a cliff.

We get a letter. It's a thick wad of pages and more pages. Here's the first sentence:

> I hereby offer you a home mortgage loan of the principal capital sum and the interest incumbent upon it quantified in Part 1 attached, subject to the condition that the home mortgage loan

is and, for the duration of the term of the home mortgage loan specified in Part 1, will be secured by a first legal mortgage charge for present and any further future advances payable to the Bank over the property specified in Part 1, and to the parties' identified in Part 1 acceptance of and compliance with all Conditions, requirements in advance of Drawdown and the General Terms and Conditions detailed in Parts 2, 3 and 4 in that order.

What a shock. It seems just as things are getting serious, the tone changes suddenly from customer language to bank language. Just as the bank has us held by our direct debits, it reveals its true character.

What Liam and Rachel experience in that moment is at least inconsistent; at most, it's linguistic schizophrenia. It has now become their lasting experience of the Bank of Kate. They are devastated by the sudden change in tone, and the fear and mistrust it causes.

Liam and Rachel know I write for a living, so they show this to me. As we chat, I want to know more about why it has had such a dramatic effect on them.

To help them come to terms with the disconnection in the letter, I ask them to imagine the type of person who wrote it. Is it a man or a woman? – A man, they guess. What age is he? – Mid-fifties. What does he do? – He's a lawyer.

I ask them to dig deeper into their imaginations. What sort of car does he drive? – An Audi, BMW or Mercedes. What sport does he play? – Golf. And the sport he follows is rugby.

All of this illustrates that he is certainly not the type of person at the stage in life where he is taking out a mortgage.

The surgeon

Now, let me be the surgeon in the title of this chapter and dissect the language, open up the nuances between the lines so that you see how the heart struggles to beat, how the tendons pull awkwardly, how the nerve ends jar.

This sentence from the bank is just the beginning of many words on many pages. From the start they have a vibe, a voice. Every set of words that strings itself into a sentence takes on a tone. That's why I asked the couple to put a face to that voice, to describe the tone.

At Dark Angels we take this idea of tone to heart. We believe that certain words, in a certain sequence, have the ability to connect the writer to the reader. Call it tone of voice, call it customer-based language.

Words have the power to connect. Or not.

This is a big paragraph for one sentence: 113 words from beginning to end means you've lost the thread of meaning by the time you reach the end. 113 words of legalese packed tightly behind the bars of a pin-stripe suit.

Our lawyer who wrote this letter to Liam and Rachel starts the sentence with 'I', yet this faint glimpse of a genuine human is quickly dissolved in the vat of heartlessness that follows.

The elephant

Here comes the elephant. The sentence is grossly overweight and overbearing. You can hear it announce itself from afar, trumpeting its own importance. Its clauses are the wrinkles in which definition gets stuck, festers and rots; the conditions like tusks, all up-front and menacing.

It fears the little mouse that can dab full stops into sentences.

The map-maker

The sentence points us to a string of other locations here, there and everywhere. Are we supposed to stop at the side of this road to read the obscure signposts? This paragraph is the equivalent of Anaximander's map, the first ever of the known world, drawn by an ancient Greek. We can see an outline; it looks like a map, but not of something we recognise. We can't follow it and it's not much use.

The road-paver

Our journey from the beginning to the end of this sentence is paved with abstractions, those big nouns that are difficult to visualise – *principal, advances, duration, acceptance, compliance, requirements* and *conditions*. They trip up the rhythm of understanding with capital-lettered speed-bumps on the road to meaning.

These words are jargon, bank jargon. Strung together they obscure the way thick hedges on a winding country road hide the view. This jargon evades clarity and deludes the writer into inflated self-importance, yet it is clumsy and ugly.

The passivist

In his delusional ignorance of how he actually sounds, our lawyer friend exposes his ego. His brief reference to himself is self-important and the only active voice in the sentence. You the customer are confined to being passively subject to *acceptance of and compliance with* the conditions. A mortgage is a big deal, yet you're not clear what your full responsibility is.

Even the mortgage itself (an inanimate object incapable of independent action and thought) gets some passive actions to perform. That action ends up being an act of rather Catholic-sounding self-restraint and bondage: *the mortgage loan being secured by a first legal mortgage charge.*

I could go on, so I will. There is so much to analyse in this one example.

Although we have guessed a lot about the man behind the mortgage, there's no clue here as to the human. Behind good writing is a heart beating with humanity, sincerity, empathy, humility and truth.

Yet this paragraph is distant, anonymous and aloof. The human evades us behind a template, hiding its action behind nouns that might easily be verbs.

Our lawyer friend wants us to take action, but we're not sure what he wants us to do. We all get through life by persuading others to act. We beg parents for permission; we talk ourselves onto our playmates' teams; we ask someone to dance; we message them for a date; we interview for a job; we offer a hand in marriage. In each of these moments we win acceptance, affection and love by being honest and real.

Why can't we do that in business writing? Why, when we go to work in a corporate institution, do we hide meaning and action in obscure words and vague phrases?

And here is the biggest effect this single sentence has.

We might be able to forgive the formality, the abstraction, the over-reliance on nouns, the complexity, even the lack of brevity. Maybe we could live with the obscurity, the capitals, passivity and flatness.

But we cannot forgive or forget the effect it has on our emotions. Reading this, Liam and Rachel felt daunted, afraid and very much let down by everything that had come before. They felt threatened.

Yes, of course it's a seriously big transaction, but the bank that behaves with warmth and respect in one moment is following it with cold calculation the next. And nothing that Liam and Rachel have done has caused that shift.

Let's stop here and change the scene.

What if that horrible letter they received was rewritten to be consistent with the experience Liam and Rachel had had up to that point? What if it started:

Dear Rachel and Liam,

We heard you have plans for a new home. It must be a very exciting time for you. You're almost there.

For our part, we're now making a formal offer of a mortgage. Our offer is subject to the conditions that we have set out in the following pages of this letter. Our offer stands for thirty days and if you decide within that time to accept it, you have six months from the date of this letter to take up the loan.

There are a few important details you'll need to know about the loan we are offering. All of them are on the next page.

There are also a lot of details attached to this letter, so we have listed the contents here:

Part 1 has more details about the mortgage loan we are offering you.

Part 2 is about any special conditions to the offer.

Part 3 tells you what you need to give us before we give you the money for the loan.

...

How come this letter sounds so much better? Besides being consistent with every experience our two young friends have had, the vibe is better and the tone of voice is dramatically different.

Let's again imagine the type of person who wrote this letter. Without showing Kate's name, I ask Liam and Rachel to ignite their imaginations. They decide a woman in her mid-thirties wrote it. She drives (rather than plays) a VW Golf and she does Pilates. She's around the same age group as Liam and Rachel and she's using their language to empathise with them.

It seems like a woman is writing. The opening lines serve no function other than to create tone. There's natural warmth and emotion there.

Just like the previous letter it gets quickly into conditions, but it does so in a firm, conversational, adult way that's collaborative – 'We'll do this, if you'll do that.' That tone builds trust, and trust is the best way to get your reader to volunteer action.

The conditions it sets are clear and unambiguous. The point-by-point signposting will definitely get the reader to where they want to go as quickly as possible and they'll know what to expect once they get there.

There's a sense of apology about the level of detail in the letter and that self-awareness seems to endear the bank to the customer.

Liam and Rachel will read this document. It invites them in. The letter sits them down and is the written version of a cup of tea and a rather nice biscuit over a serious chat about their future.

It gets to the point in their own everyday language. There is none of that clichéd language here, no 'as you are aware', 'in relation to', 'further to my previous correspondence', no 'I am pleased to offer you', no 'please do not hesitate to contact me' and no 'please note'.

It's all transparent, conversational, connective language.

There's little doubt there's a human being with a sentient, beating heart at the other end of this letter. It feels authentic, objective, self-confident, warm, with just a touch of humility – enough to demonstrate respect.

We can't claim this new letter is creative, that it uses techniques like a compelling opening or unexpected verbs to entertain its reader. It's a bank letter, after all.

But consider this...

If Liam and Rachel had not seen the expensive TV commercial, if they had not met with Kate, this letter would have been their one and only experience of this bank's brand. And what a poor first impression a letter like that can make.

When you count the richness of marketing budgets available to banks and insurance companies, and add in the abundant skills they have in checks and balances, it's frightening to realise how much of their shareholders' money they might be wasting by ignoring the inconsistency in their communications.

As their ad airs on TV and the marketing department count up their views, likes and retweets, customers are likely opening a humdinger of a bank letter at the same moment: the type of letter written by our middle-aged lawyer friend.

That's the moment the budget fades into thin air. And the effect is invisible to those who are bean-counting that budget. Like as not, those letters issue automatically under cover of darkness. They are sent overnight from an automatic system that spits out letters by the thousands.

If you work in communications in financial services, remember one thing (though this advice might apply equally well to most other kinds of business): every piece of customer communication you produce is part of a story you tell your customers. It's got a tone, a vibe and a voice. Make sure it connects with everything else you write to them. Spend well. Write well. Connect well.

Try this

Pick up a piece of communication from a bank or insurance company. Not an ad, but a day-to-day communication about an account or policy.

Now imagine you had to speak the main message in that communication. How would you convey that message if you had to phone someone about it? How would you convey it at home to your partner?

Write down the words you would use over the phone or face to face – the words you use when you speak.

Now compare what you've written to the communication you started with.

Different, aren't they?

Clearer, shorter, more natural and human.

Enough said.

8

Why do I do what I do?

The off-the-top-of-my-head answer: I don't know. The back-of-the-matchbox answer: because it's a living. The frowning, careful answer: because I don't know what else I could do. And the real answer? Because there is nothing else I want to do.

In both business writing and in fiction, I write for the enjoyment of spinning a world. Of chasing the next thought. Capturing it. Sometimes I imagine myself as a Victorian entomologist, spending sepia-toned days quietly pinning insects to cards.

I use words to make sense of the world, and myself. And while these words don't always need to make the same sense to anyone else, it's immensely gratifying when they do.

Some days, I have no answer to the question, nor do I need one. It's just what I do.

Henrietta McKervey, copywriter and fiction writer

TS&CS, SANS LEGALESE

CRAIG B. WATSON

If you'd like to skip this chapter, that's fine. Just sign below.

> I have read and understood this chapter and agree to its contents.
>
> (Signed) _____ (Date) _____

Great, thanks. See ya! Enjoy the one on annual reports.

But what if there's a Rumpelstiltskin clause? Will you be like one of the six Londoners who agreed in 2014 to relinquish their firstborn for an hour's free WiFi? Or one of the 22,000 Mancunians who signed up in 2017 to 1,000 hours of community service?

It's always a risk. And you have to weigh it against the absolute certainty that you'll waste your life if you *do* read everything.

So why read a chapter on Ts&Cs (terms and conditions)? Maybe I should explain why I wrote one.

Apart from periods prancing around in a periwig, I've spent most of my career working as an in-house lawyer with banks, life offices and asset managers. A good deal of this has involved reading contracts, legislation and regulation, much of which could've been better written.

There are two saving graces to doing this in a professional capacity: I get to be grumpy about other lawyers, and I get paid for it. But when I'm expected to read sloppy Ts&Cs as a consumer, I just get grumpy.

Everyone hates the small print. Yet we're content to put up with any old dross provided:

it's been churned out by a lawyer,

we're not compelled to read it, and

there's somewhere to sign, or a button that says 'I AGREE'.

And now, when practically every website and every software update demands a confirmatory click, humanity's biggest, fattest collective fib must surely be, 'I have read the terms and conditions.'

You'd think that, after quarter of a century in the study and practice of law, I'd have reconciled myself to this reality – to the pages and pixels of turgid terms, confusing conditions and downright dreary drafting that are presented to us on a pretty much daily basis. You'd think that, after all the trimming, tweaking and tinkering I've tried over the years, all the splenetic soliloquising, I'd have come to some sort of grudging acceptance that nobody reads the stuff, so it's hardly worth getting het up about.

I'm not there yet.

Ts&Cs shouldn't be an imposition. Folk shouldn't have to suffer this click-through charade. And if we're writing something that's significant enough for people to be bound by, we should have the courtesy to write it well.

Here's my attempt to explain why legal writing can be so bad and how it can be so much better. It's a chapter for lawyers and anyone who's ever moaned about them.

All legal writing depends on a single quality. If that quality is lacking, the writing will be 'bad'.

That quality is: clarity.

Legal writers may lack faith. They almost certainly lack hope. But if they lack clarity, they have failed.

An old tutor of mine used to put it something like this: 'Legal drafting is the art of expressing yourself in such a way that no one can be in any doubt as to what you actually mean.'

Like all good writing, it is indeed an art. It's an art in the old-fashioned sense of requiring long study, much practice, keeping abreast of developments and needing to be sure of what you're doing before you start breaking the rules. But it's not an art that offers fame and fortune, even to those performing at the highest levels. After all, the truly great legal writer is only doing their job.

If done well, the work goes largely unnoticed, except by wise old souls like Miss Maudie Atkinson who summed things up nicely when she said of Atticus Finch in Harper Lee's *To Kill a Mockingbird*, 'he can make somebody's will so airtight can't anybody meddle with it.'

If there's no room for misinterpretation, there's no room for dispute. And there are few more valuable things a lawyer can do for her client than keep him out of court.

But legal writing is hard, and the people with the necessary skills or desire to draw up legislation or contracts are in short supply. As a consequence, those tasked with turning out page after page of unassailable prose are often deluged in work and deprived of time. Blaise Pascal once excused the length of a text he'd written by saying he didn't have time to be more succinct (and because he made the mistake of saying it in French around 1657, the quote was subsequently attributed to all manner of people, including Mark Twain who probably never said it at all. Still, Blaise got the credit for Pascal's Triangle which had been around for centuries, so it all evens out). Here's one reason why statutes, contracts and standard Ts&Cs are so lengthy: it takes longer to write shorter.

If you're writing Ts&Cs, there are two ways you can save on time: 'swerve it' or 'swipe it'.

Swerve it. Decide you don't need it. Avoid having to write it in the first place. Decide what's important and what goes without saying. You need to know what you're doing here, but ask yourself:

What am I hoping to achieve for my client by writing this?

What risks am I trying to mitigate?

What does the reader *need* to know?

And, if you really want to save time, ask:

Does the law already provide for this?

Take consumer contracts, for instance. There's a whole raft of legislation that serves to protect consumers and to make it difficult for businesses to avoid their responsibilities by pointing to the small print. If you're an online retailer, you need to tell customers about their rights to return goods and about how you're processing their personal data. Beyond that, there's not a great deal to be said. So why say it? Why stuff your webpages full of legalese when it's not going to reduce your obligations to your customers – or your potential liability – one whit? And if your products or services happen to be more complicated, isn't it better to save your efforts for explaining how they work?

My friend, Cindy, has a business that makes and sells herbal teas. As a medical herbalist, she knows exactly what should go in her teas. She was less clear on what should go in the Cindy's Teas Ts&Cs. She asked me what she could say to protect her business. I told her, 'Very little.' I explained that you can't avoid liability for personal injury, nor can you prevent someone from making a spurious claim in court. But you *can* convey information that might be helpful to your customers. Eventually, I managed to boil things down to:

Drinking this tea is not a substitute for seeing your doctor!

It's clear, it's succinct, it conveys a serious message with a bit of humour, and it fits well with her brand. It doesn't alter the default legal position, but it's a more positive message than the equally ineffective alternative:

Drink this tea at your own risk.

The trouble is, we've become so used to seeing voluminous sets of Ts&Cs that businesses feel obliged to have them. In a business-to-business context, where parties are generally free to negotiate changes to the default legal position between themselves, Ts&Cs can be important. But in a business-to-consumer context, they often do little more than annoy the customer.

Not always, though. As online Ts&Cs go, the Google Terms of Service are short and clear. They say several things that technically don't need saying (such as, 'You may use our Services only as permitted by law' – duh!), but whoever drafted them has obviously given thought to what customers might want to know. Here's an example:

Some of our Services allow you to upload, submit, store, send or receive content. You retain ownership of any intellectual property rights that you hold in that content. In short, what belongs to you stays yours.

William Morris said, 'Have nothing in your house that you do not know to be useful, or believe to be beautiful.'

For consumer contracts, I say:

Have nothing in your Ts&Cs that you do not know to be essential, or believe to be helpful.

This leads to the second way you can cut drafting time: swipe it.

When it comes to contracts, plagiarism is positively encouraged. Very rarely does anyone start completely from scratch. If your client needs a software licensing agreement, you dig out a template, or borrow a colleague's, or find one online or in a book. It's rather like a novelist who sits down to write a fantasy novel and pulls up a tried-and-tested fantasy novel opener:

> In a hole in the ground there lived a hobbit. Not a nasty, dirty, wet hole, filled with the ends of worms and an oozy smell...

By the time you're done, fewer than half the words will be ones you've written. For some standard form agreements, chances are you've only changed names and addresses:

> Mr and Mrs Furzley, of number five, Primrose Drive, were proud to say that they were perfectly normal, thank you very much...

Since there's no Oscar for Best Original Contract, you can pinch and pilfer as you please. But, again, you need to know your stuff. The cardinal rule for using templates is: don't put anything in a contract unless you understand what it means and why it should be there.

This takes knowledge and experience. And some of the time you save in the writing you'll spend in the editing. There are precious few shortcuts to doing a good job.

Doing a half-arsed job is easy, though. All you need is a stack of templates and a fear of leaving stuff out. Templates themselves have a tendency to expand. With each development in the law, there's always an adding, seldom a taking away. Besides, it's quicker to keep than to cut.

Don't be a slave to the template.

And, if you see anything you can improve, tweak away. Can any of those boilerplate clauses that you've read dozens of times before be made more user-friendly? Remember, any changes you make to the template will serve you both now and next time. Reduce, reuse, recycle.

Once you've discerned the useful from the useless and trimmed your template right back, you can start adding in the stuff that applies to this particular job. You'll need to know your client's business, or product, or whatever it is you're covering in this set of Ts&Cs. Many lawyers don't take enough time to understand what their client does and what's important to them. Take that time. Be curious. Collaborate. (And if you're the client, don't think you can leave it all to the lawyers.)

Then, when you have a fair idea of what needs to go in, get writing.

Unfortunately, the usual glib advice like 'write from the heart' doesn't apply to legal writing – or to many lawyers, for that matter. Writing from the head will suffice. Think about what you want to say. Get those thoughts down. Agonise over how you might say it better. And remember, your prime objective is clarity.

How do you ensure clarity? Read. Re-read. Read it out loud. Leave it for a bit. Come back to it fresh. Get colleagues to read it. Read bits out of context. Take a leaf out of Atticus Finch's book: put yourself in the shoes of the reader and walk around for a bit. Whose shoes? Your client's. Those of your client's customer or counterpart. Or opposing lawyers. A judge. The appeal judges. The generations of law students who'll read the case report in years to come and laugh at your incompetence.

You'll need clarity at all levels, from the overall message and structure right down to the fine detail.

In my third year at high school, I did a work placement with a local solicitors' firm which led to a regular gig doing the mail on Friday afternoons when the office junior was on day-release to college.

Back at the dawn of the 1990s, all the letters and deeds were dictated into Dictaphones and typed up on electric typewriters. It was my job to get the resulting stack of paper signed, stuff it into envelopes, sling it through the franking machine, sort it into bags and sprint it along to the post office before closing.

Not long into my junior-office-junior role, I took some 'signing' into the cigar-scented room of one of the partners. He extended a finger towards the top corner of the bundle I was holding. 'That,' he said, pointing to a paperclip, 'is the most dangerous item in the office.'

And so he told how this innocuous-looking, curly piece of metal had got lawyers into all sorts of scrapes on account of its propensity to link things that ought to remain unlinked, and vice versa.

Its equivalent in legal writing is an innocuous-looking, curly piece of punctuation: the comma.

In the law reports, no other punctuation mark attracts such notoriety. Misplaced commas can alter meaning, as can commas that are missed or unplaced. Indeed, the lack of an Oxford comma meant a Portland-based dairy company was held liable to pay its Maine-based delivery drivers overtime at a cost of $5 million. Under a provision of Maine employment law designed to discourage dawdling in the perishable goods industry, overtime was not payable for:

The canning, processing, preserving, freezing, drying, marketing, storing, packing for shipment or distribution of:

(1) Agricultural produce;

(2) Meat and fish products; and

(3) Perishable foods.

The delivery drivers argued that 'packing for shipment or distribution of' should be read as a single task, not two separate ones, and that driving the delivery vehicles was eligible for overtime. In accepting their argument, the court observed that an 'Oxford' (or 'serial') comma would have made all the difference.

But the decision need not spell despair for Oxford comma detractors. There are several other ways the original intention could have been made clear, such as losing 'for shipment', changing the order of the tasks, or altering the layout to show the activities in a numbered or bulleted list. Or you could do what the Maine legislature did in the revised version:

> The canning; processing; preserving; freezing; drying; marketing; storing; packing for shipment; or distributing of…

Note the substitution of semi-colons for the commas, and the insertion of a semi-colon where the Oxford comma might have been. Note also the replacement of 'distribution' with 'distributing' which reflects another geeky discussion from the case about how all the other tasks in the list were gerunds. Clearly, the Maine legislature has addressed the lack of an Oxford (or serial) comma by taking a belt and braces (or suspenders) approach.

That was a dispute over the interpretation of sloppily drafted legislation. There have been many similar disputes over sloppily drafted contracts. Commas have caused such havoc in the lives of legal writers and their clients over the years that there grew an ill-advised fashion for abandoning their use entirely. But reading a clause or two of a document drafted in line with this philosophy will soon convince you that one seldom finds clarity in a comma-less contract. Joyce dedicated several dozen pages in *Ulysses* to demonstrating that punctuation is – on balance – a blessing.

I learned the finer points of punctuation in my final year at primary school. My teacher used to hand out typed sheets containing a long passage without a single capital letter or punctuation mark. We had to copy it into our jotters, inserting the correct punctuation. It was an exercise I disliked because I couldn't fathom how I was supposed to get the right answer when there were so many possibilities. Of course, there was *no* single right answer – only good and bad choices.

We also had to write down and observe the following 'rule': Never start a sentence with And, With, But, Or or Because.

'Or what?!' I thought. And still do. With some rules, there are exceptions. But others may be ignored completely. Because they're silly.

Rules are made to be br…

…*iefly glossed at the end of a chapter that's pushing its word count…*

'Keep it brief,' they say. Absolutely! But don't sacrifice clarity for brevity. If you need more words to make it clearer, use them. Use as many words as you need. But no more than that.

'Avoid jargon,' they say. But jargon can be fine if everybody uses and understands it in exactly the same way.

'Avoid legalese,' they say. If they mean using 'hereinbefore' and 'in the event that', then definitely. Either find a list of substitutes or just try to sound like a human being. But if they mean using precise legal terminology, ignore them. Use the precise terms.

'Use "shall" to denote obligation,' they say. A worthwhile convention if you're drafting a lengthy contract which refers to the parties in the third person. (If you're using 'we' and 'you', it's 'we will' and 'you shall'.) But if your Ts&Cs are short, conversational and consumer-focused, then saying 'you shall' repeatedly is going to sound stuffy and domineering. Should you persist, you'll only get into a spat with your marketing folk about 'tone of voice' – which you'll lose.

'Rules is rules,' they say. Fair enough. But in legal writing, all rules and conventions are subordinate to clarity.

One more rule: when you think you're done, force yourself into doing a final check. You won't want to. You'll be thoroughly bored with it all by now. But you're *bound* to find something.

And, when your Ts&Cs have gone to print, or are posted on a website, you'll have the peculiar satisfaction of knowing that your carefully crafted clauses are out there being skipped, skimmed or scorned by hundreds, thousands or even millions of readers.

Maybe some will give your words more than a glance. Maybe they'll concede, 'That wasn't so bad.' You seldom find out. But in this line of work, success is having made the effort.

Try this

Some years back, my daughter wrote down the three rules she would make if she were queen for the day:

1. it mit
2. wer clos
3. bi nis

You have supreme legislative authority to make three rules of two words each. Write them.

9

I live in my own world of thoughts and ideas. We all do.

I write to see if those ideas can take off by themselves. It's only by writing that I can give them air and lift.

Standing back to read whatever I've scribbled is when I discover whether they can actually fly. (The hope being to leave business language on the runway and let real engagement take the reader's imagination skywards.)

The day I stop writing would be to ground my day's fleet of thoughts. I would be locking them in a hangar. Unthinkable – and unliveable with.

Will Awdry, advertising writer turned creative director

LET THE WRITER WRITE

ON WRITING ANNUAL REPORTS

CLAIRE BODANIS

Imagine you're an architect – or a builder. You have an exciting new project – a new building in central London, with a strict deadline but a really nice client and a relatively generous budget. Sounds pretty good, doesn't it?

Then you read the requirements, and they go something like this:

A cosy, two-bedroom cottage (local sandstone essential), with a view of an oak tree and a stream from the kitchen window (roses round the door optional).

A pumping station using the latest in modern pipework, systems and automated technology; must be able to deal with $xxxm^3$ effluent per day.

A twenty-storey block of flats, ten flats per floor, must include 20 per cent social housing.

I am exaggerating just a little to make the point, but in essence, this is the central problem faced by those tasked with writing and producing annual reports. The requirements are so wide, and often seem so contradictory, that it can be difficult to know where to start.

But as a writer, you have to start, because starting is the one inescapable writing imperative. You have to start because you want to do your best for your clients. That's the obligation for any writer in the business world. But you also have an obligation to yourself and your craft because, as a writer, you can influence *how* that happens. You want to amaze your client that you managed to do so much with this seemingly impossible brief. It's the perennial, joyful aspiration that motivates us all.

So, yes, the annual report must meet all the regulations and tick all the boxes. But it should tell a story. It must explain how the company 'creates value for all its stakeholders' – but legally, it's a document for shareholders. It should tell you why the company is a long-term investment proposition – and confirm that it's still going to be in business in three to five years – but it must present the financial results for the current year.

It should be concise and readable – but it must contain all the financial statements, and the detailed remuneration report and (every three years at least) the remuneration policy, which, for most FTSE companies, will mean you're up to a minimum of 120 pages already before you've even started writing anything else. In among all this, the annual report must be, by law, 'fair, balanced and understandable'.

And that's just what the Companies Act, the Corporate Governance Code and the Financial Reporting Council are telling us. If you also consider that the annual report is the one corporate document that has to be audited, approved by the Board, published by law on a certain date and requires information from every different part of a company, then you can begin to see why they are so often held up as some of the worst examples of corporate communication. Boring, uninspiring, confusing, badly written. Of course, the question is, 'Does it have to be?' There's a challenge for any writer. But the regulations are firm as well as voluminous.

As one FTSE 100 annual report manager described, 'Increasing regulation is resulting in more and more disclosure, adding more and more clutter. It's even worse for those of us with listings elsewhere, as we need to address sometimes conflicting requirements. It comes down to the regulatory burden versus telling a good story.' Or, as summarised by a director of communications, 'How do you make it comprehensive while also being short and pithy?'

Does that mean we should just give up and not bother even trying to do them well? On the contrary – writers love a constraint, after all. True, it would be easier with fewer, and perhaps less contradictory ones, but that just makes it more interesting. Because the truly inspiring thing about annual reports, which makes them so worthwhile, and which has kept me interested for nearly twenty years, is precisely that they are so important. At what other time does a corporate writer get to see into the minds of a company's leaders? At what other time are we given the opportunity to hear not only about a business but, often, about a whole sector, from those who really know what they're commenting on?

It's because they are pored over by everyone, lawyers included (more on that later), that annual reports become the 'source of truth' for a company. People inside and outside the business know that what's in the annual report has been sanctioned, so you see its words popping up all over the place.

A sad thing writers hear all too often is, 'No one reads the annual report anyway.' Well, that may be true, if we are talking about first-to-last-page reading of the report. But whether it's bad or good, the information that's in it will be read somewhere, even if not in its original pages. If it's written badly, then bad writing will abound. But if it's done well, then what can be more satisfying for a writer than to see their work travelling all over the place? And it's this multiplying effect that makes it even more important to write annual reports as best we possibly can.

So, what does 'writing as best we possibly can' mean in practice? From a FTSE 250 comms director: 'The biggest challenge when writing an annual report is to find a way to explain what a company does, and how successful it is at

117

doing it, in a clear and simple way that can be understood by someone who has never come across the company before. It sounds easy enough but it's difficult to do, and the temptation to resort to "corporate speak" or generic terms is strong. But the best annual reports find a way to make the complex simple to understand.'

Another described the communications challenge: 'Who is the report aimed at? Depending on the answer, the style of writing may vary – and if there is more than one audience, then how do you pitch it?'

And there's the perennial problem of multiple contributors, as a government report-writer commented: 'The most challenging issue is when a report is authored by several people. You have to … handle sometimes variable quality or style in drafting and edit the final document so there is only one voice telling a story that keeps the reader engaged.'

I think we can all agree, then, that writing an annual report is not easy, which is why so many companies ask a professional writer to do the job. Those – often smaller ones – that don't are frequently confronted by the challenges described by one company secretary: 'The authors are usually internal members of the team who are already very stretched in their roles. They are often not particularly skilled at telling the organisation's story in a way that engages the reader, as they are too close to it and their skills lie in other areas, not annual report writing! So it's a challenge to pull everyone's contributions together in good time to enable a thorough review, and sometimes a rewrite.'

So, the answer to the 'how to write the annual report' question is, hire a writer and that's the job done? Would that it were so simple. Engaging a good writer is just the first step. The annual report is a process-driven project like no other. And, because it's a legal document, the many different people responsible for their own contributions are nervous and cautious in a way they wouldn't be with anything else. If you don't get the process right, that beautiful first draft produced by the writer will bear little, if any, resemblance to what appears in the published report.

But the process isn't about ticking off steps in a project plan. It's about bringing all those contributors along with you. By the end of the project they should feel that hiring a writer was the best thing that ever happened – not just because the document is better, but because it was easier and less work for them. They should love their writer.

So how do you make that possible? Start by laying the groundwork early on in the process. It's crucial to define and agree the brief, explaining what you are doing, why and with whose authority (particularly if you're bringing a writer in for the first time – but it never hurts to remind people). And give your contributors examples of the kind of writing they can expect to see.

Unless a company has just had its IPO (initial public offering), and this is its first report, people will be used to a way of writing, a way of doing things. And new people coming from other companies will be used to their way of doing things. If contributors haven't really understood the purpose of the report, they won't want to change how they are used to writing for their own internal audiences. From an annual report manager in a pharma company: 'Another difficulty is cutting through the internal jargon, and, in a company like ours, the technical and scientific terms. As contributors tend to know their areas well, it is often difficult persuading them that they need to use different language.' And, when problems arise, as they inevitably will, if contributors haven't bought into working with a writer and don't trust them, they'll rush back to the old way, because they can at least be sure that they won't get into trouble for doing so.

What a good writer brings to the task is a clarity of thinking that exhibits itself in clarity of writing. The writer will express the essence of the company – addressing key issues of purpose and performance – through phrases that are stripped of the worst jargon. Of course, jargon is often a way of hiding – of being deliberately unclear – but the writer has also to be the business's conscience.

In a sense the writer is the linguistic auditor. The writer's words need to be as clear as possible because this document will become 'the source of truth'. That's a responsibility, and the best clients recognise that and listen hard to their writer. Respect develops on the basis of words, words that have real meaning. That is a positive challenge for all involved. And sometimes or often, because the process will dictate decisions, the writer's words will be changed; but at least everyone will understand why.

Great. Hire a writer, get the contributors to love their writer, and all's well? Not quite. One thing we haven't mentioned is that annual reports are not – or shouldn't be – written like books. Why? Because people don't read annual reports like books – they flick through them like magazines, and read what catches their eye. So annual reports, despite their book-like size, should be thought of more like magazines – magazines that deal with complex subjects, but present them clearly, in an engaging and interesting way. *National Geographic*, perhaps, or *New Scientist*.

Enter the designer. And this is where the skill of the writer (and the designer, but we're focusing on writing here) really comes to the fore. It's hard enough to write straight narrative that's engaging and interesting, but the best annual reports are the combined output of the designer and the writer, a seamless visual and verbal interpretation of a single, shared idea. Design is there not to look pretty but to illuminate content, to amplify the message. And you can only do that by working together.

Too many companies keep their writers and designers apart (and too many writers and designers let them do it). The result is uninspiring design and flabby writing – in short, the kind of report that you're lucky if anyone even looks at, let alone flicks through or reads. So, if you're at the commissioning end, bring the team together and let them work together. Insist that they work together. And your annual report will be better for it.

Think of that well-known saying, 'A picture is worth a thousand words.' It's so well known that we don't really know who first said it. But there is the riposte by Bill Marsteller, 'But not necessarily worth one word. The right word.'

Now, we're nearing the end of the process. All the contributors are happy. The report looks great, and is a good read. Surely we've done enough? Unfortunately not. There is one group left that could still sabotage our beautiful work. Yes, we all love to hate the lawyers, those destroyers of the well-turned phrase, those killers of linguistic beauty. From a Fortune 500 company reporting director: 'Balance is a key principle, and requires the company not only to talk about the positive achievements of the year but to be transparent about its negative impacts, too. This is something lawyers get nervous about. The writers may try, but it's not uncommon to find a report falling back into impersonal language when talking about controversial issues. You know when the lawyer has provided the script.'

What do you do? Be brave. Do the right thing. The lawyers are your advisors, not your masters. As long as what you're saying isn't legally wrong, and you haven't made a mistake, say it anyway. Most of what lawyers advise companies not to say are the very things that everyone wants to hear – the unvarnished, unspun truth. People aren't stupid. They can tell when you're trying to hide something. And these days, when things are so difficult to hide, why bother? You'll get a lot more credit for being honest.

So, let me summarise. To produce your best annual report, in five clear (I didn't say easy) steps:

Engage your writer.

Define the brief – what you're doing and why – and make sure everyone involved understands it.

Bring your contributors along with you – let them love their writer.

Allow your writer and designer to work together – or better, insist that they do.

Be brave, and rein in the lawyers.

In short, let the writer write.

Try this

Five steps to a great brief

(thanks to John Simmons)

The idea of a story can give us the structure for a creative brief, where the desired outcome of the brief is the clear telling of a story. Any form of communication can be thought of as a story – including an annual report. If you're commissioning an annual report, try this yourself to create your brief for your writer. If you're a writer and haven't received a proper 'story' brief, try writing it yourself and presenting it back to your client.

Take one of the oldest stories in the world, Homer's *Odyssey*: it can be broken up into five parts, as seen from the viewpoint of Odysseus.

Problem: 'I need to find my way home through unknown seas.'

Doubt: 'I'm weary, I'm lost, I'm scared.'

Exploration: 'I just have to sail and keep sailing, having many adventures, as I look for my home island.'

Resolution: 'Eventually I will find my wife and home by displaying great courage.'

Celebration: 'Then I'm happy again.'

Questions about the expectation for each stage in the story can help create a response to the brief that produces better storytelling.

Question 1: the problem

What is the one unmistakeable outcome you want in response to this brief?

This gives us a headline statement that sets out the issue and the PROBLEM to be addressed.

Question 2: the doubt

What are the main questions that arise from probing that headline?

This clarifies the issues in DOUBT that need to be thought of as a challenge.

Question 3: the exploration

Who are the people we're really trying to influence and what are the obstacles to overcome?

There is a need for a thorough EXPLORATION to get us closer to the answers.

Question 4: the resolution

What answers are we really wanting to find?

This will enable us to recognise the RESOLUTION when we find it.

Question 5: the celebration

What will be the result of a successful resolution?

This will mean that we can CELEBRATE the outcome.

If you apply the discipline of allowing yourself only a single-sentence answer to each question, you can provide a summary that sets out clearly the expectations of the brief in the form of a story.

PART IV

Staying True to Yourself

10

Why am I a writer? I've no choice; it's all I can do. It's all I want to do. It keeps me alive, in every sense. When it stops being a challenge, I'll stop being a writer.

Roger Horberry, brand writer, author, trainer and non-musician

BEING PURPOSELESSNESSLESS

ANDY MILLIGAN

At President John F. Kennedy's inauguration in 1961, Adlai Stevenson told the crowd that in classical times when Cicero had finished speaking, the people said, 'How well he spoke,' but when Demosthenes had finished speaking, they said, 'Let us march.'

Demosthenes understood both the power of a purpose and the power of persuasion. No matter how good your purpose or how strongly you feel about it, if you cannot turn it into words that will move an audience, it is purposeless. Kennedy knew this, too, and his famous speech announcing the ambition of America's space race, 'We choose to go to the moon ... not because it is easy but because it is hard', is a masterclass in persuasive purpose.

Purpose needs to be accompanied by persuasion. That means you must take care of the words in which you clothe it. A great purpose should inspire action. But it will only be persuasive if written in language that can move the crowd.

First, what do we mean by purpose as distinct from vision or mission? The Oxford Dictionary definition of purpose is that it is 'the reason for which something is done or created or for which something exists'; whereas vision is defined as the 'ability to think about or plan the future'. You can see from those two definitions why purpose is the more compelling concept, the more inspiring word. Even the sound of it – the two 'plosive' Ps – suggests energy and direction.

Many people in business can be confused by what purpose means in the context of their organisation. Too often it is regarded as a statement of corporate social responsibility, an important adjunct to or part of the business but not the core of the organisation. Others can be confused by its apparent similarity to vision or mission.

Purpose, in a business context, is distinct from vision and mission in the following way. A vision statement sets out what the organisation wishes to be like in the future; it is a description of its ambition for itself. Usually it includes adjectives like 'world-leading'. A mission statement describes what kind of business the organisation actually does or what it is, usually with some reference to a specific type of customer (often it includes words like 'solutions provider').

Purpose is motivational: not about *where* the organisation is heading or *what* the organisation does, but *why* it does it. And to be motivational it has to be outwardly focused, describing the impact the organisation wants to have on the lives of its customers, society or the world at large.

Purpose differs from vision and mission in another way, too. A purpose, in an organisational context, is an enduring motivation that does not have an obvious endpoint. This is unlike vision or mission. Vision describes a future state that you will reach at some stage – at which point you may well need a new vision. Mission defines what you are currently doing and may change along with your vision. But purpose should not change, unless there is a significant change in your business, because it responds to a continuing need. For example, the BBC's purpose has been since its inception to 'inform, educate, entertain'. That purpose will be as relevant tomorrow as it is today and as it was decades ago.

There are two elements to a well-written purpose. One, the content. Two, the tone of voice. The first gives the message; the second provides the persuasion. Together they create meaning.

In terms of content, a good purpose will:

- Describe how the organisation does good for the customer

- Describe how the organisation does good for the world in which those customers live

- Be credible because it is congruent with the core competence or capabilities of the company

- Drive action

- Motivate the people inside the business

- Be enduring

Any of the above can be done explicitly or implicitly, but you must be able to explain how the purpose meets each of those criteria.

For example, Google's original purpose *was* 'to organise the world's information and make it universally accessible and useful'. It doesn't explicitly state who the customer is, because it is obvious that the customer is every one of us. Implicitly and explicitly, it meets each of the criteria for a good purpose.

Agreeing the content or message of your purpose, the enduring need to which you respond and which motivates your organisation, is difficult. It is, though, far easier by comparison than agreeing the tone of voice – the words with which your purpose is written. And unfortunately a great purpose may well be made underwhelming by poor writing.

Here are some tips on how to get the tone of voice right.

1. Be as precise as possible. Find a word or phrase that anchors your purpose in the reality of what you actually do or the greater benefit that your work provides. Don't make it too general or vague. Nike's purpose is not 'help people realise their potential' but 'to bring inspiration and innovation to every athlete in the world'. The words 'every athlete' are carefully chosen for a sportswear company. There's a kicker here, too, as Nike define 'athlete' as follows: 'If you have a body, you're an athlete.' It's their irreverent way of explaining that they are targeting an attitude or mindset, not a specific or narrow demographic.

2. Avoid loose or vague terms, especially words like 'integrity', 'world-class' or 'respect'. And above all, please avoid using 'passion' or 'passionate'. These are attributes or values that should be apparent in what you do; they aren't motivators for why you do it. The purpose of WWF, for example, is 'to help people find ways to live in harmony with nature'. It's clear that they need to act with integrity, respect for the natural world and people and with the passion for a cause to deliver that purpose. They don't need to write those words into the purpose.

3. Find a word or phrase that causes conflict within your team or that provokes discomfort. If something is to be remembered then it must provoke a reaction and emotion, even a negative one. Some people will feel uncomfortable with a strong word because they fear it will alienate somebody. Let that debate rage, but ultimately, when the dust has settled, make sure the word that has caused dissension is the one that you use. Otherwise the purpose will be bland and not memorable. Let's take an example: one of my favourite purposes is that of the hotel group IHG. It has the deceptively simple phrase, 'great hotels guests love'. It's a fine rhetorically balanced phrase. It has rhythm and ends strongly. The word 'love' was deliberately chosen. It would've been easier to use the word 'enjoy' but using the word 'love' forces the organisation to think more purposefully about improving the quality of the experience they give guests. It is intended to encourage them to take the time to understand exactly what it is a guest would *love* rather than just *like*.

4. Ask yourself, is this different from that of any of our competitors? If it isn't, then either your purpose is not that compelling, or you are writing it in a way that is hiding its true power. For example, here are three purposes, each from a different bank:

> To help people fulfil their hopes and dreams and realise their ambitions

> To use our skills and resources to enable others to achieve their goals and dreams in the home lives and in the businesses

> To help people achieve their ambitions – in the right way

There is nothing wrong with any of these purposes, and indeed there is an attempt to introduce language that might not necessarily be associated with a bank ('hopes and dreams', for instance). However, there's not much to separate them, either in their content or their tone of voice.

Compare them with this purpose:

> To make going to the bank the best thing you did all day

How ambitious is that? It conceives the customer not only as someone who needs to use a bank, but as someone who can choose to do many different things during the day. Suddenly this bank has decided to compete with visiting shops, bars, cafés, restaurants, cinemas – maybe even just having a walk in the sun. That is Umpqua Bank's purpose. Umpqua is one of America's most successful banks; in fact it is one of America's most-loved brands. They sought inspiration for their bank experience not from other banks but from other retailers, including fashion designers and coffee shops. They are a 'community bank' and so create an atmosphere of community in their branches, with the likes of free coffee and local musicians playing. They wanted to be dramatically different from any other bank and reflected that in the words they chose for their purpose. You can imagine how many other banks would struggle with choosing the phrase 'best bank', let alone 'best thing'. But at Umpqua they resolutely embrace it, and it also informs their behaviour and tone of voice more generally. The former CEO, Ray Davies, insisted on everyone answering any telephone call with the phrase, 'Welcome to the best bank in the world.' They even gauged people's comfort level with saying the phrase as a litmus test for hiring.

5. Beware of poetic licence. The use of metaphor, simile and other literary devices has its vital place in the role of communication – particularly in communications with your customers and your employees. But your purpose is a dangerous place to use them, because what you are aiming for is crystal clarity. You need to be able to communicate your purpose to everyone so they understand its relevance. And you need to avoid the 'snigger factor'. Uber's purpose is 'to make transportation as reliable as running water, everywhere, for everyone'. Really? 'Running water'? Is that what motivates an Uber driver? Is running water even really reliable? Everywhere? Moreover, does that tone of voice sound true to Uber's identity? Do we see such metaphor or word-play in the company's other communications, or in any part of its customer experience? I'm not aware of any, and I am a loyal Uber customer.

Compare that with innocent. They are known for their playful, witty tone of voice. Metaphor, analogy, simile are all regularly used to amuse and engage customers and colleagues, who often use playful language in response. But innocent's purpose is admirably free of any such literary devices. It is to 'get the best food and drink into the widest number of people and places'. There are no metaphorical flourishes in that statement, but it feels authentic to innocent and certainly ticks the criteria of a good purpose.

6. Finally, be succinct. Aim for the fewest words you can. Avoid writing the purpose by consensus. If you do, you will surely find yourself putting more words in just to please a few more people on your board or committee. Brevity is a virtue. Zappos, the online shoes and clothing retailer, reduced their purpose to two words: 'delivering happiness'. Both words were carefully chosen to reflect an online retail business from which customers bought things that they desired, and which employed people who would go the extra mile with a smile to ensure they got them. They built a culture to create a great brand experience that made both customers and employees not merely satisfied, but happy. You may not be able to be as concise as that, but keep it as short as possible while using the most provocative and prescriptive words.

Here are a few other purposes written in ways that I personally admire.

IBM was given its purpose by Thomas Watson over a hundred years ago – to develop 'information technologies that benefit mankind'. These farsighted words have guided the business through many different iterations over the years. From typewriters to computers and now beyond any physical product at all, IBM has always looked to develop information technology that benefits mankind; or as their recent advertising slogan put it, to find solutions for 'a smarter planet'.

Ingvar Kamprad founded IKEA 'to create a better everyday life for the many people'. The words do not explicitly specify what IKEA sells, and that's because IKEA is a greater idea than its products. However, its category of goods is implied, because 'everyday life' involves things like tables, chairs, cupboards, shelves, bookcases, beds, sofas, carpets, cutlery, food, drink etc. IKEA makes them all to be desirable in form and function, and affordable to almost anyone.

The purpose of the UK-based budget hotel chain Premier Inn is best articulated in the promise to give guests 'a good night's sleep, guaranteed'. There are two keywords here: one is 'good' and the other is 'guaranteed'. Premier Inn operates a guarantee-based business model – like Domino's Pizza and their thirty-minute delivery guarantee. If you do not enjoy a good night's sleep, they give you your money back. Premier Inn have hardwired the purpose into the business – which is much more than many companies do.

Which leads me to another point about purpose. Your purpose needs to be accompanied by some clear promises. Otherwise, how does anyone know how it will be turned into practice? Customers require something that they actually experience and through which they understand and appreciate what your purpose is, even if they never know or articulate its precise wording. In order to deliver their purpose, Premier Inn had to make good on their key promises – by, for example, offering the Hypnos bed, which is a six-star hotel bed in a budget hotel. Clearly a great bed is the starting point for a great night's sleep. But the promises are also met with a friendly, easy and convenient welcome and very good air-conditioning that doesn't disturb your sleep. Even the BBC, with its aspirational purpose to 'inform, educate and entertain' has to accompany that purpose with promises. Recent examples include to 'transform our offer for young audiences' and 'develop a more personal BBC', to reflect changing audiences and take advantage of new digital technologies that allow greater choice of viewing or listening through a whole range of smart devices.

Purpose must be turned into practice. The starting point is to persuade your employees of your purpose. Inspire them, motivate them, direct them to do something every day that will always be relevant to your customers, and will improve their lives and the world in which they live. Use words, as Demosthenes did, that make people want 'to march'.

Without clarity of purpose and persuasive language, businesses will drift, employees become unmotivated, customers become dissatisfied and eventually companies even collapse.

Finally, I will leave you with the words of Sir Marcus Browning MP. Perhaps his is the most persuasive articulation of both the importance of purpose and the perils of not having one:

Purpose is what we are striving for. We must have purpose. We mustn't be purposeless. We mustn't exhibit purposelessness. We must be purposelessnessless. Because we don't want to end up, do we, like the blind man in the dark room looking for the black cat that isn't there.[1]

1. As told by Rowan Atkinson.

Try this

A great purpose is often found in the reason your (or your client's) organisation started in the first place. In the cause that gave it life. If the organisation's founding purpose has been consigned to the attic of corporate history, it might be worth getting it out and dusting it down to see what it tells you. What did the founders really stand for? What did you really stand for, if you are the founder? What was the vision for the organisation that was being created? What struggles did people go through to achieve it? Try retelling that story for now, and see if it refreshes your thoughts about what the organisation is doing and where it's going. See if it helps reconnect you and your colleagues with your sense of purpose and each other. The author E. M. Forster famously exhorted, 'Only connect.' Sometimes to rediscover the persuasive power of your purpose, you need only to reconnect.

11

Why do I do what I do?

Because writing things down is the only way I know of really thinking things through.

Nick Parker, writer, formerly at The Writer

READERS ON WRITING

MARTIN LEE

There are as many great writers today as there always were, but many fewer great readers.

Gore Vidal

I'm starting this chapter with a quote I don't agree with. To qualify that, I agree with the first half of it, but not the second half. I'm including it because it shows that great writers (or at least one of them) are concerned with the quality of reading that is going on. And if we're going to have a book about business writing, then we should devote at least one chapter to the act of reading. After all, for all that there may be hundreds of people who can call themselves business writers, every literate person in the country reads our output virtually every day of their lives. We need to know what they think about it.

The first thing to say about these readers is that they are experts. Because they've been reading business writers' stuff since primary school, they are extremely skilled at it, without realising just how good they are. But when you ask them a direct question about a piece of copy, even people who did hopelessly at English will know straightaway if they are reading something that has integrity and/or utility. And why. Therefore, writers need to understand that they have a highly experienced and demanding readership that needs to command their respect. A novelist might pull a fast one on a reader; a business writer won't. And of course, they shouldn't want to...

In my day job, I spend a lot of time listening to readers (members of the public) talking about the efforts of business writers to be persuasive, and over time, all that listening has taught me a lot about how readers think, and the rules of thumb they bring to bear on our writing.

I'm going to share some of the most important and recurring rules of thumb in this chapter. These are the things that I hear people saying time and again, which leads me to the simple conclusion that writers should take note. If you hold these principles close, you won't go far wrong, and you'll improve your chances of writing in a way that is both useful and satisfying to readers.

1. Precise writing is trustworthy

Nothing irritates readers of business writing more than vagueness. Not only is it irritating, it's a warning signal. Correctly, readers' instinct goes like this: if this business could be specific about a claim or a product quality, then they would be. But because they've been woolly, it's dodgy. So, a vague claim is a bogus claim. Here is specificity in action:

Look at that writing at the bottom: '100 night trial | free delivery | £75 off with code SLEEPRICH'

This is writing that is profoundly trustworthy. There are the precise number of words needed to convey the offer, and there's no shifty writing to decode or interpret. It's impossible to misconstrue. Well done, eve mattresses.

It's also true for corporate apologies. Businesses make mistakes, and sometimes they make serious errors of judgement. VW did, for example, but they got their apology right as far as readers are concerned.

We have broken the most important part in our vehicles: your trust.

Now, our number one priority is winning back that trust.

We know that actions speak louder than words. So we will directly contact every customer affected and resolve the issue for them.

If you have a 1.2, 1.6 or 2.0 litre diesel Volkswagen or Volkswagen commercial vehicle, it may need attention.

If you have an EU6 diesel engine, V6 TDI or V8 TDI, or any petrol engine, you are not affected.

To find out if your vehicle is affected, visit:
volkswagen.co.uk
volkswagen-vans.co.uk

In the meantime please rest assured that all our vehicles are safe and roadworthy and that we'll continue to do everything we can to win back your trust.

What readers like in this ad is the specificity about which models are affected by the exhaust emissions scandal. There is an absence of airbrushing here, an honest admission of being in the wrong, and clarity on how it affects customers. And although the headline is clever copywriting, it doesn't shirk from the nub of the issue.

So, here are a couple of important suggestions for business writers straightaway:

Read back what you've written. Is it free of any woolly vagueness?

If in doubt, go back to your source, which may be your client, and challenge them to be as specific as they can. It isn't in anyone's interest – yours, the client's or the reader's – for anything vague to see the light of day.

2. Readers don't read until you've finished, they read until they've finished

And here's the thing: they nearly always finish first. I don't wish to be brutal, but readers are not as interested in your words as you are. Their preoccupation is getting back to their lives as quickly as possible. So if you have written a piece of copy about something they need to know, they typically don't read to the end – they read until they believe they've understood it sufficiently to stop reading.

Let me illustrate this with reference to the shortest of all types of business writing. In our company, we are often asked to test taglines for brands. It is common to be given up to half a dozen to test with members of the public. They tend to vary in length from three words (occasionally) to up to ten. Almost every single time, readers choose the one with the fewest number of words, regardless of rhythm or meaning. Why? Here are some verbatim responses:

'That one, because it's shorter.'

'I can't remember a long one.'

'I can't be bothered with one that long.' (It was five words long.)

'I'm not interested enough to read a long one.'

Now, a competent reader can read 200 words a minute. This means that the time saved in reading three words rather than six is a fraction over one second, but they'll take that saving. That's how little investment they'll put into your words, and how much more they value the alternative way they could be using that second.

So, although I happen to believe that lines like 'Just do it', 'I'm lovin' it', or 'Every little helps' are fine examples of brand lines (partly because their brands have stuck with them for years, incidentally), it's clear that their success is also down to their brevity.

The implications of all this are not difficult to grasp.

Write the fewest number of words you can.

Put your most critical words first.

3. How it looks matters as much as what it says

This is going to be painful for writers to read, but it's true. Again, as part of my job, I'm frequently handing people a piece of copy to read and then watching them read it. The client typically wants to establish a selection of these:

Is it clearly written?

Does it feel relevant to them?

Do they know what action they need to take?

Will they take any action?

Are they happy with the tone of voice? And what tone does it evoke?

Does it make the reader feel warmer towards the brand?

Now, what you invariably observe when you hand them the specimen copy is that they don't simply launch in and start reading. They give themselves a split second to make a swift visual sweep. It's like a personalised early warning system. They are trying to manage their own expectations. The question they want to answer is none of the above, but actually, 'Do I *believe* that I will find this easy to read?' And the clues to that are in the layout and composition. If it looks dense and impenetrable, they believe that the reading experience will be, too. If it's airy and visually attractive, they assume that the writer, plus designer, have thought about the reader and gone to the effort of making it look appealing.

What this all means is that by the time they start reading, they've already made up their mind about whether it's likely to be digestible. You *might* change their mind with your actual words, but in my experience, that instinctive impression is definitive most of the time.

4. Ensure the reward is worth the effort

Both of the previous points are leading up to this one, and I realise that I'm breaking my own golden rule by not putting my most critical words first. However, I am gambling on the hope that in your case, you actually are invested in reading to the end (and of course, if I'm wrong, you've gone already).

It's very important that we don't think that readers are somehow lazy. A more respectful and more accurate way of thinking about them is that they crave efficiency. You're no different. You rarely take the longest route if there is a quicker and easier way to get to your destination, because in most circumstances, you're looking for the most efficient one. But you might, if there was a reward to the slower, harder journey, such as beautiful scenery.

The same is true of readers of business writing. They are looking for efficiency, too. And when faced with a piece of writing, they make an intuitive judgement: what reward am I going to get out of this in return for the effort I have to put in? And here's the thing: they don't want to finish reading it to find out that the effort/reward equation didn't stack up. They want to estimate it in advance.

Not convinced? Reading books for pleasure is the same, and you'll do this, too. I used to be a bookseller, and in the case of fiction, say, you could watch customers browsing, making a swift judgement based on the cover, and then perhaps thinking, 'Yes, that's the kind of book I've enjoyed reading in the past.' Then they pick it up, read the blurb on the back, perhaps riffle through the pages, read the first sentence or two and then make a decision. All of that was a calculation of effort and reward. And that is perhaps why I've got no memory of ever having sold a copy of *Finnegans Wake*.

I'd go so far as to say that this intuitive exercise is a vital skill for all humans. If we didn't develop expertise in these types of estimations, we'd never be able to transact the basics of living a life. And of course, we really do make these judgements continually when reading. People who buy a paper don't get all the way through the sports section and then say, 'I don't know why I did that – I hate all sport, which reading that section has reminded me.' Instead, they use their learnt efficiency to line the cat's litter tray with the sports section instead.

5. Make it easy to compare to other types of communication

This point I've been stressing about efficiency is seen in another psychological principle that comes into play when we read. In the language of behavioural economics, this principle is called 'anchoring'. It makes use of the fact that readers

147

immediately compare what they've got in front of them with similar communications that they are used to; this mentally prepares them for the type of judgements they are likely to make. We're all very used to anchoring at work – it's when film posters say things such as, 'If you liked X, then you'll love Z.' X is being used as an anchor to sell Z. The advertiser is essentially controlling how we perceive their offer rather than leaving it up to us to make sense of it.

Now, all readers of business communications have anchors available to them. In practice, most bits of writing fall into one of a number of buckets, and we instinctively sift any new bit of communication accordingly. Below are some of the common ones that readers have seen time and again, together with their learnt expectations of this genre of communication. It's meeting that standard that they want from your writing.

Out now – date-specific information for one-offs (gigs, books, films, theatre, sale starts, etc). As simple as it gets.

New edition (e.g. ISA season, bonds, annual releases) – often comes with new claims that need to be compared with previous versions. The essential differences, highlighted with specificity and transparency, are what the reader is looking for. A subset of this is 'new and improved'. How is it improved? Be clear and straight with the reader.

Brand new – could be in any category, but we're talking about a claim of genuine innovation. From a reader's point of view, it's nearly always a question of 'How will this make my life better/more pleasurable/easier/more efficient?' So make that abundantly clear. Put the benefit fully in the reader's terms, rather than from the perspective of the brand/service provider/manufacturer.

Product descriptions – a lot of what people read isn't about new things so much as items they want or need, such as replacement items, presents for people, etc. Of course, you're allowed to enthuse and be proud of your products, so appealing to the emotions is entirely permissible, but don't forget that people also crave accuracy. How heavy or wide is it? It doesn't matter how fulsomely you eulogise if I don't know if it will fit in my bathroom.

Vital changes – often true of public sector communications. If a behaviour change is mandatory, then the reader must know instantly. They've learned to look for this straightaway. And any such behaviour change is nearly always date-specific. Make this immediately clear as well.

We're sorry – sometimes for a monumental corporate cock-up, like the VW example earlier, but typically for something less catastrophic but still irritating, like a data breach or admin blunder. Deal with this by being honest, specific, straightforward about how it will be corrected, any implication for the customer and what you've put in place to prevent a recurrence.

Discretionary reading (e.g. newsletters, brand or relationship-building communications and so on) – some of the most complex stuff. Bear the effort equation in mind. The reader could be doing something else with their time instead and is indulging you/the brand here. Be crystal clear in your mind about the type of reward you want the reader to get before you start writing. Modern tips like 'three-minute read' work well here – signal the commitment up front.

6. Be wary of too much 'tone of voice'

Very few readers love overly intimate tonality in business writing. It tends to feel suspicious, especially when necessary information is being communicated in long copy. You're not their friend, and if the tone oversteps the mark, it can evoke the kind of reaction similar to when someone invades your physical personal space. If you're writing for a brand that has a very intense, emotional relationship with its customers, there is more permission, but if you're in any doubt, keep a more respectful distance. You're normally trying to be a midwife to a product, service or important piece of information rather than building a personal relationship, and readers will thank you for keeping it that way.

Having said that, this isn't the nineteenth century. Readers today are happy with a tone that you might think of as 'relaxed formality'. A sentence such as, 'We're writing to you because there's been a change in the law regarding how your data is used,' is far better than, say, 'It may have come to your attention that under the provisions of the Consumer Data Act...' It's also better than something more unbuttoned such as, 'We know that this is one of those terminally dull letters that you're tempted to screw up and throw in the bin, but bear with us because this is one you've sadly got to read.' The problem with this is that while you're exercising your tone of voice, you're also wasting their time. Don't do it; it's disrespectful.

7. Remember, it's all about trust

I'm going to finish where I started. The vast majority of the business writing you will do is designed to be persuasive. Readers know this. And as a result, they are in a semi-defensive posture all the time. Why? Because, quite simply, they have to reject most of the attempts at persuasion they encounter or they'd go bankrupt.

For this reason, the essential trustworthiness of your writing is always its most important quality. The trust of customers or users is one of the most valuable assets any organisation or business can gain, and if you are writing for them, never lose sight of that. Readers are subliminally sniffing out trustworthiness on a continual basis and have a number of mental shortcuts that they deploy. I'll list those in a minute, but where trust in organisations is concerned, the most important principle is the same as it is for trust between people – do they have my best interests at heart? Any organisation that is convincing in this regard has something of enormous value. Writing that communicates that quality is beyond precious. Therefore, bear these reader-based principles in mind. I make no apology for repeating myself:

Is it specific? If it is, I can believe it.

Is it simple? If it is, I know they've got nothing to hide.

Does it look good? If it does, it makes me think they care about it and want me to read it.

Is it concise? If it is, then I know they aren't wasting my time with unnecessary waffle.

Is it free of errors? If it is, I know they have paid attention to detail.

If your writing passes all these intuitive tests, readers start to relax into it. At some instinctive level, your writing will strike them as genuine and human. They won't consciously praise it, but in fact it will be something better than that. It will have an invisibility to it, because it's not drawing attention to itself so much as connecting readers directly to the product, service or information that you are writing about. Without having to strive for effect, you'll be believable and useful. And, if I may speak on their behalf, they'll be grateful.

Try this

In order to bring the principles in this chapter to life, it's worth trying the following exercise.

Make a commitment to read the next unsolicited marketing email that drops into your inbox in full. Every word of it.

Follow through on the commitment. Go on, the whole thing.

Make notes about how this process makes you *feel* – don't worry about the content of it; capture the emotions. If you're like me, you may start to feel a sense of creeping irritation that rises to a crescendo of blind rage. Skipping might feel like a biological necessity, but resist that impulse.

Now go back and rewrite the email with this brief: all it has to do is leave you personally feeling engaged, informed and satisfied.

If you get the chance, share the experience and the two versions with a colleague or friend and see what impact the two have on them.

Make a note of what you've learned from the whole exercise and make a couple of personal commitments to your own writing.

12

Because I've been hooked on language since I was exiled down south from Lancashire at the age of five. Suddenly I was defined by the way I spoke.

Because big, boring business has a duty to communicate better with the rest of us. And I can help them.

Because those moments when a bit of writing raises a smile – or even just an eyebrow – are brilliant.

Because it's a cheap thrill to see something I've written on the side of a van.

Because training people is fascinating. It's often not really about writing, but questions of identity, education, values, corporate culture. I get to pretend to be a psychologist.

Because very few people get the chance to turn the thing they're really interested in into the thing they do every day. So I'm lucky, and grateful.

Neil Taylor, brand and language consultant, founder of Schwa

WRITER IN THE CORPORATE WORLD

NEIL BAKER

My brief is to tell you something useful about writing in the corporate world. My first thought is that I probably can't add much to what's been said elsewhere in this book. It's a book, after all, about writing for people; communicating well with people through the medium of words. The corporate world is comprised of people and organisations, which are just conglomerations of people. Why does it need its own chapter?

What's different about writing in the corporate world is, I think, nothing and everything. To make my point, I'm going to do something we don't normally do at Dark Angels. I'm going to lay down some rules. Five of them. Oh, and before I start, a brief caveat: there *are* people in the corporate world who care deeply about words, who value good writing and who are great writers themselves. I've been lucky enough to work with many of them. If you're a client of mine, don't be alarmed by what follows. I'm not talking about you. Honest. Now, read on...

1. Don't be boring

Rule number one is as simple as this: don't write boring words. Don't create boring stuff. I don't think I need to elaborate, but I will, just in case, as this is the most important thing I can share with you.

If you were writing in any other context – writing a novel, for example – the need to not be boring would be obvious. But in the corporate world, the risk of tedium can be overlooked. When a communication fails, the explanations I hear include:

people have short attention spans these days; nobody watches more than the first seven seconds of a video; this audience doesn't read.

No, no, no.

The way we access and consume information is changing. The way we work is changing. But face this fact: if people don't 'engage with your content' it's probably because it's boring.

What do I mean by boring? You know what I mean. Boring is the opposite of interesting. It is…

Arid, colourless, drab, dreary, dull, dusty, flat, ho-hum, humdrum, jading, jejune, leaden, monochromatic, ponderous, slow, stale, tame, tedious, uninteresting, wearying.

I've led planning workshops where we've brainstormed why the thing we're creating might fail to connect with the audience. The hope is that if we bring these risks into the room up front, we can avoid them. Very sensible. Here are some of the pitfalls people often write on the little sticky notes I hand out: we might use too much jargon; we might not have enough facts to back up our argument; we might try to create something that we can't afford, or something that will take too long to produce. All good problems to be aware of. But remember this one: we might create something that's boring. That's the big one. If it's boring, the audience will ignore it. They have better things to do with their time.

So I'll say it one last time, at the risk of boring you: please, nothing boring.

2. Work out what you are trying to say

I've been working as a writer for thirty years. Since the start, I've been editing other writers, too. In all those years, there's one question I've asked more than any other: what are you trying to say? (Often followed quickly by: why would anyone care?) I ask that question before I start to write anything, while I'm writing and when I'm editing. (I'm asking it myself now, as I write this sentence and as I go on to the next paragraph.)

When I moved out of journalism and started working with organisations large and small, helping them to tell their stories and share their ideas, to write and communicate better, I kept asking the same question. I've read the brief, yes, but what are you trying to say? I've digested the brand strategy, yes, but what are you trying to say? I've battled my way through your 147 PowerPoint slides, but what are you trying to say? Beneath the jargon, the woolly thinking, the vainglorious boastfulness and even – whisper it – the bullshit... what are you trying to say? And why would anyone care?

Here are two reasons why the quality of writing and communication between people in the corporate world can so easily become dispiritingly abysmal:

1. People are unable to say what they want to say; and
2. They don't know what they were trying to say anyway.

It's essential to acknowledge that these are two related, but different, problems. If you don't know what you are trying to say, your communications will fail – regardless of how skilled you are with words. You can try to fancy up the language, paper over the cracks with jargon, make the tone fresh and friendly, bring in a more experienced writer to help, but it won't be any help, unless...

Unless you acknowledge this paradox: you can't write well unless you know what you are trying to say, but the best way to work out what you are trying to say is to jump in and start writing. Fumble about, go off at tangents, take wrong turnings, retrace your steps, charge on ahead. Know that the only way to arrive at the place you need to be, which is the point at which you know – or think you know – what you want to say, is to try to say it. Only then can you go back and rethink, restructure, rewrite until it works.

Every piece of writing emerges from a messy, iterative process that can look horribly inefficient. In the corporate world, inefficient mess is a Bad Thing. In the corporate world, every step must be a step forward. This makes writing difficult. So, what can I say that's helpful? Perhaps only this: know that this is how good writing takes shape. Explain this fact to the people you work with. When a draft is nudging closer to sign-off, and other people have reviewed it and said it's fine, but you have a nagging feeling that now – why only now? – the mists are beginning to clear and you are starting to glimpse what your words should really be saying, be bold. Have the courage to ask one last time: what am I trying to say? Why would anyone care? And if the answers mean you have to start again, then start again.

3. Don't (always) get straight to the point

My favourite film is *Star Wars*. Or maybe *Lost in Translation*. It depends what mood I'm in. For the purposes of this rule, let's say it is *Star Wars*. (And I deliberately call it *Star Wars*, not the awful new title it was given for the millennial generation, which I won't dignify by typing here.)

Depending which source you trust, *Star Wars* is the biggest grossing movie of all time. Adjusted for inflation, it's raked in $1.5 billion. When it was released in 1977, it was the original blockbuster, because people queued around the block to see it. Morons. Why didn't they save their time and money by asking someone who'd already seen it to tell them about it? Imagine this:

'Hey, have you seen *Star Wars* yet?'

'Yes, it's incredible.'

'I'm busy – what's the key point in one sentence?'

'An evil empire builds a fearsome weapon that can destroy whole planets at the push of a button, so some other people blow it up.'

'Really? I don't get what all the fuss is about.'

You've probably heard something like this a million times: 'We're targeting busy leaders in the global logistics industry. They are time-short. You have to get straight to the point.'

Well, yes, you do sometimes. But not always. (See the rule about not being boring.) Sometimes it can be better to take a less direct route. Sometimes you'll want to put the most important thing you have to say right at the very end. Sometimes you'll want to tell a story.

But don't overdo the storytelling. Sadly, it's become a cliché in the corporate world. Everyone wants to talk about narrative. That's fine. Stories can be powerful things. But if I'm staying in your hotel and the roof is on fire, I don't want you to tell me a ramblingly hilarious story about a middle-aged writer who was asleep one night in a hotel that caught fire, even if I find that story so engaging that next time I stay in a hotel (once I've been released from hospital) I'll be sure to check where the fire exits are located, and I'll tell everyone I know to do likewise. No, I want you to kick down my door and say this: 'Get out now. The roof is on fire. It's this way to the stairs.'

Let what you want to say shape how you say it.

4. Always have a point worth getting to

If you don't work in the corporate world, this rule might sound a bit strange. Why would you try to communicate something if you don't have anything worth saying?

Usually, because you've been told to. Example:

'The leadership team had a meeting last week. Can you write something about it for the newsletter?'

'Sure. What did you agree?'

'Nothing, really.'

'What did you discuss?'

'We can't say anything about that.'

'What should I write about then?'

'The mood was very constructive.'

'Do people need to know that?'

'No, but we're committed to transparency.'

I try to work only with clients who have a genuine desire to communicate something. Sadly, that's not everyone in the corporate world. It might look like they are trying to communicate, but in fact they are doing something else entirely. Often they are speaking their brains, boosting their egos, ticking the boxes, positioning themselves for promotion, passing the buck or just making noise. Sometimes their motivation is impossible to discern. You can't write well for these people, or help them to communicate.

All I can say here is if you care about writing and communication, work with and for people who also care – or who are, at least, willing to be persuaded of its value. Otherwise… well, life's too short. If you can write and communicate well, you have a talent. Please don't waste it.

Which brings me to my final rule.

5. Do no harm

What's your favourite word? Mine is oblong. I like the sound it makes, the way it feels in my mouth. The round and bouncy 'ob', the languorous 'long', the blurting 'bl' that joins its two syllables. I associate the word with happy maths lessons at school. I'm talking here about the late 1970s, early 1980s. We had circles, triangles and squares. We had a multiplicity of polygons. And we had the family of quadrilaterals. That included the rhombus, the trapezium, the kite and my favourite, the beloved oblong. In my childhood there were no rectangles. It would be hard to fall in love with the rectangle. I think 'retch' or 'rectum'. 'Angle' is sharp and, well, angular. It has the feel of an aggressive, bullying word. At some point – I don't know when, why or how – rectangle elbowed out oblong. I ask my children to draw an oblong and they can't. They don't know what I'm talking about. Oblong gone.

Everything I've written in that paragraph might be historical nonsense. Perhaps rectangle has been around much longer than oblong. Perhaps oblong is thriving today, but I'm asking the wrong children to draw one. I don't know and it doesn't matter. The important thing is that I love the word oblong, for reasons that run deeper than its dictionary definition.

Reflect on what your favourite word might be. Perhaps its meaning appeals to you. 'Glisk' is the perfect word for a stream of sunlight through a cloud. The act of picking up litter while out jogging is beautifully, necessarily, 'plogging' – not because the 'plo' comes from the 'plod' of a slow jog, but because it's rooted in 'plocka', which is 'to pick up' in Swedish, where this environmentally friendly exercise emerged. That's lovely, isn't it?

Words give us so much more than their literal meaning. They have a feel in the mouth, a tune in the ear, a look on the page or screen, a set of associations, a sense of character, a story to tell, a voice of their own, a place in the heart. Learn to receive the pleasures that words offer. Enjoy writing, of course. The meaning-making that occurs when individual words are strung together into sequences of sentences and pages of paragraphs and endless threads of connections that help us make sense of our lives is magical. But love words as individuals, too. Spend time with them, through reading, thinking, speaking and writing. Become their friends. Not so you can make better use of them, although that will happen. But so you can look after them, nurture and protect them. I am not exaggerating – or not exaggerating too much – when I say that, for me, words are living things, with beating hearts. When I see or hear people misusing them, abusing them, being unkind to them, I am pained. It hurts me when people hurt words. Our shared language, our ability to tell our stories, communicate our ideas and connect with each other suffers.

Everyone who writes – not just those of us who call ourselves writers – should try to write as well as we can. When we become friends with words, that process can, perhaps, become a little easier. Writing is less of a chore, more of a game we play with our friends. But we have a responsibility to those friends: to protect them, to stand up for them.

I don't mean we should become nit-picking auditors of grammar, syntax and diction. My premise is that words are living things, so it follows that we must allow them to grow and flourish, to experiment with new ways of being in the world. What I mean is that we should care for words as a doctor would care for her patients. Doctors swear an oath to do no harm. As writers, let's do likewise. Let's care for words as well as we can.

That 'as well as we can' is important. There is only so much a doctor can do for her patient; sometimes, it is a losing battle.

The patient suffers, or even dies. As writers in the corporate world, we experience the same failure. There is sometimes – or often – only so much we can do. We will encounter people who do not share our love of words. Working out of confident ignorance, they will lobotomise our language, wreck our words. The worst will hurt them on purpose, torturing them into unnatural turns of phrase. They will do things to words, with words, that are cruel and inhuman. But if we have taken our oath, we will do the best we can to stop the suffering. And always, we will do no harm.

Those of us who do care must stick together and support each other, because the road can be tough and lonely. Ask around, inside your organisation and beyond. Find your tribe. The ability to write well is a wonderful, powerful and valuable thing. Protect it, nurture it, celebrate it.

I'll end with a quote from Gabriela Mistral, the Nobel Prize-winning poet: 'Speech is our second possession, after the soul – and perhaps we have no other possession in this world.' What I'm trying to say is this: writer, mind your language. Words are all you have and everything you need. So stand up. Stand by your words. They matter. They are your friends. *Viva la* oblong!

Try this

- My pledge is 'do no harm'. What's yours? It might be the same, or you might prefer something of your own. The important thing is to take a pledge. Write it down. Sign it. Try to live – and write – by it.

- You will encounter people who don't care about writing and don't understand it. But sometimes, what they say goes. It can hurt. Find people who *do* care. Spend time with them. Encourage each other, learn from each other. Make your shared values a source of strength.

- Sometimes you might have to write about things that are a bit, well, boring. How can you make it interesting? Maybe you can't. But here's what you *can* do: you can become interested in the challenge of making it interesting. Even that little sprinkle of interesting will make your writing better. If you're bored, your reader will be, too. If you're interested, there's a chance your reader might be.

- Writing at or for work can be creatively rewarding. Why not? But it isn't always. Don't get fed up when it isn't. Don't expect too much from it. Keep yourself creatively engaged through your own writing projects. You don't need to get published or win prizes, although you might; who knows? Just make some time to play with words. As Isak Dinesen advised, 'Write a little every day, without hope, without despair.'

A selection of writing by Dark Angels alumni

Over the years since our first Dark Angels course in 2004, our alumni have written hundreds of 'personal pieces' that they read out on the final evenings of the courses. They apply the skills and techniques discovered – and the sense of liberation – to their subsequent writing at work. Here we show a small selection from a variety of Dark Angels courses.

A FRY-UP

ROB WILLIAMS

The tea's already come and the toast's already gone. So yes toast is first speaking strictly but it isn't really and anyway, he's eaten it now. Why? Because he was hungry, that's why. So tea is first today.

Grey and brown with something black bobbing on the café's reflection. He doesn't remove it. He accepts it. Accepts everything here, but only here. Only that which forms part of this ritual.

Rachel, barely sixteen and basted in grease yet still attractive the way wasted beauty is attractive to long-time would-be heroes like him, presents him with his plate.

'Enjoy, Harry…'

Enjoy. That's part of it, certainly. Nowhere near all of it.

He eyes the platter with confidence. Blobs lumps of brown and lays lines of red sauce next to the sausage and over the bacon. You do not touch the egg. As he thinks it he catches his own fractured portrait in separate puddles of fat like minor coastline disasters pooled in the lowlands of his heaped plate. He has his best blue jacket on, he remembers, with the open-necked white shirt. Looking smart, son. Handsome Harry. The way he looked for Sunday lunch when he had a job all the week. Well.

A vast gulp of tea swallows the black thing and it has no taste. He rocks gently to his left and chances a silent fart. Picks up the cold heavy knife and fork. He's ready.

Truth is anywhere's fine to start; within reason of course. But you do not touch the egg. Bacon then. Fine. A square of brittle bacon skimmed through beans made substantial by fried bread and a generous cluster of mushrooms. Next is sausage, sausage is next and it's no good pretending it isn't. His knife bursts the skin exposes pink innards and his fork halves fried black pudding that tries to crumble but is grouted with brown and then bean sauce; a skilled tradesman at work now. Tomato next obviously, definitely. The tinned tomato is the bladder of a football he had as a boy that his brother burst not with a fork but with a penknife. Bastard. He told him black pudding was made of pig's bollocks and—

You can wink at me… I know you're there. Egg is last, you know that. It's tits first. His brother told him that too.

He wasn't right very often.

Next Harry, next. Concentrate. More fragile rusty bacon good choice Harry, good choice, tactical; lubricated with tomato and mushroom and OK just a shard of egg white now – dropped onto the fried bread. You do not even look at the yolk. A half smile and the grease is cold on his lips; mug slippery at his mouth. The craftsman working steadily across the cooling landscape and getting there, getting there; the plate becoming fluid, the bread a mop, the bacon a snowplough for errant beans and mushrooms, colours disappearing – all things become one. All things become brown.

The last veiny sack of tom. The final mouthful of swine's testicles. Oh I see… you…

Nearly there.

Reverently he transplants the untouched yolk onto the surviving square of golden bread. You then use whatever remains sausage-wise to pick up most but certainly not *all* of the surrounding sauce. Do not for God's sake make that mistake. You can spoil everything, even now. Especially now. I'm coming for you…

He lays down his cutlery while he chews the sausage. There is much to be savoured now. The last lumps of pork banger; the short belch in which he tastes salty bacon for the second time in mere minutes; the first whiff of the fag that will accompany the lukewarm dregs of his tea; and above all this: this perfect yolk that's been waiting here for him for what seems like a week. *Is* a week, in fact.

It's the anticipation that is truly sweet; that makes him lick his lips again. Sweeter even than this sauce. Anticipation not only of the yolk but also of the end. He can taste that too now. It tastes of nothing.

Steadying the island of fried bread with his fork he slices easily into the centre of the yolk through the bread down to the scarred porcelain and his heart clenches. The day halts, then the tension leaks from him just as this toddler's painting of a ripe yellow sunshine leaks its rays in all directions, bleeding light and spreading life until all form is lost. He eats quickly now: loudly, messily, gluey thumb pushing fried bread round like an inelegant ice skater soaking up every last trace of sticky sun and sugary brown slurry.

And then it's gone.

He drops the cutlery and leans back in his chair. Immediately he can hear his heart calming, settling.

Emptying.

'Alright, Harry?' Rachel checks, a gnawed thumb already on the edge of his plate.

He almost nods.

'What are you doing today then, Harry?' she tries, just as she tries every Saturday morning; and she suspects – just as she suspects every Saturday morning – that once the silent old wolf in the yolk-stained blazer has devoured his fry-up and smoked his fag, he has absolutely no idea what he's going to do next.

Written at Moniack Mhor Foundation course in the Scottish Highlands, in 2006. At the time Rob was creative director at Penguin. He then went on to become an internationally acclaimed screenwriter of series like The Man in the High Castle *(Amazon) and* The Victim *(BBC1).*

ROWAN OAK

JONATHAN HOLT

The white columns are the cover shot,
a publisher's easy dream about the South.

The front porch is the foreword,
surprisingly brief.

The foyer is the copyright page,
there because it must be.

The staircase is the table of contents,
giving away nothing.

The crack in the wall is the family tree,
winding down toward the land.

The living room is the epigraph:
an uncomfortable quotation.

And the hallway is the first sentence
and his study is the rise before the fall
and the patio is the summer scene with the Tennessee Waltz.

The servants' house is the dirty little secret,
built with his own hands

And the kitchen is the heart of the work,
the fire that could destroy it.

And the bedrooms are the walls
the characters hide their truths behind.

And the door to the balcony is the essential paradox
and the walkway is the climax, where the girl lies dead
and the cedar rows are the ghosts that stay with you after the end.

But in the sum of it, the pages are empty
a thin flicker of alabaster

because the ink is in the cemetery
and the words are all in other books.

Written at Moniack Mhor Foundation course 2006, a few weeks after an evocative but ultimately disappointing visit to William Faulkner's house in Mississippi. Jonathan was at BP at the time, and his freelance writing career has continued since. Now back in the US, his novel nears completion.

T. S. ELIOT'S SCOUT

His vowels: round as
the curve of his bowler hat.
They say he's a Yank.

Written at Merton College, Oxford, in 2015, where Jonathan's Dark Angels journey continued.

THE SAINTS REPORT TO GOD ON ARACENA

SUSANNAH HART

We don't have much to report, Lord.
A quiet year in a quiet town,
the usual highs and lows.
We have the data tabulated somewhere,
if you like.
No? We'll summarise, then.

Early in the year, at long last,
Maria and Ricardo Garcia had a baby boy.
You can imagine Doña Felipa's delight.
The child is half suffocated in blankets.

Last Saturday, after ten years of patient waiting,
Sofia Estepona married Pedro.
Both mothers-in-law are relieved
and are handing out recipes.

The physics teacher at the high school
is drinking too much again.
It's the long hours after class he can't stand,
that, and the endless summer
when heat stamps him into the ground.

Señor Diaz, the butcher, harbours
indecent thoughts about his wife's cousin's niece.
Her skin's plump with untapped promise
and he sweats in bed at night and prays for peace.

Manuel Perez has lost his dog, poor kid,
and last week,
when the chestnut trees were burdened
with their barbed fruit, a truck ran off the road
and killed Cristina Santos.
The cobbles are hushed,
and the pale houses hang their heads.
Yesterday, they rang the bell
to send her soul to you.
Handle her carefully, Lord.
We miss her too.

What else?
We had a fine showing for Semana Santa
and the Aracenese did us proud.
There was some dispute among the Virgins
as to the most beautiful of all,
but we think we interceded amicably
on your behalf.

Well, Lord, we guess that's it.
Remember, we're here to do your bidding
and show your children right from wrong.

Same time next year?

Written at Aracena, Spain, in 2008. Susannah is a brand writer whose poetry continues to flourish. Her collection Out of True *was published in 2019.*

COMMANDING PASSION

NEIL DUFFY

Dear Neil,

Please forgive me the awkwardness and formality of this mode of communication. I could have spoken to you, but I wasn't sure I trusted myself with the words unless I committed them to paper.

Neil. How passionate are you? How passionate are you about me? This is important.

Don't you think that 'passion' is a super word? It sounds like crushed red velvet cushions or bruised rose petals. You can use two syllables, 'pa–shone'; or three: 'pash–ee–on', depending on just how passionate you feel. You can even have a 'pash' – like boarding school girls felt for their gym mistresses in the 1950s.

Now, Neil, I'm worried about you and your passion. You tell me you that you 'like me very much' – big wow!

I've done my research and feel that I now command the subject, so tell me, Neil, just how passionate are you?

First let me define for you:

PASSION
An affection of the mind;
A vehement, commanding or overpowering emotion;
A mode in which the mind is affected or acted upon, as ambition, avarice, desire, hope, fear, love, hatred, joy, grief, anger, revenge;
Amorous feeling; love; amorous desires;
Sexual desire or impulse;
An overpowering zeal or enthusiasm for some object.

There's plenty more, Neil, but I think you get my point – we're talking unreasonable, fixated, unyielding.

When you first see me, when we meet, what do you feel?

Are your feelings even nearly as heightened as Mike and Sherie Draper of Brown Drainage & Construction? They are passionate about building the best drainage team in the Waikato region of New Zealand. Does your passion for me match Mike and Sherie's unreasonable drainage fixation?

I know that you like my legs – you tell me. You like to stroke them. I like it as well. It warms me. But what do you feel when you think about my legs?

Neil – are you passionate about my legs?

The good people at the Corby Trouser Press Company are very aware of the subject of passion and their customers' fervent feelings for their trouser presses.

They make replacement feet fittings for the Corby 7000 series trouser press. These are painstakingly crafted and moulded for superior balance and weight distribution whilst operating this superb trouser press.

Available in either black or white, these fixtures are ideal for those who are passionate about their J Corby trouser press and who wish to maintain it as opposed to change it.

See: J Corby know that those crazy trouser press aficionados would rather die than abandon the crisp creases that their Corby gifts them.

Imagine that you will never touch my legs again – do you feel loss – real loss? The kind of loss that the Corby user would feel as he waved his beloved trouser press farewell on a scrap yard van? I just don't know if you do, Neil.

You have a very gentle touch. Sometimes you kiss the back of my neck slowly and smell my hair. I like this. I tingle. It touches me. When you do this I imagine passion welling inside you, until you say: 'You feel nice.' Well, thanks!

The next time you kiss me there I would commend you to think hard about the driving emotions of Doug Call, the president and owner of Virginia Prosthetics. He is self-confessed 'passionate about the prosthetics business, and maintains his skills in the profession. He enjoys making a positive impact on the lives of amputees.' That's what I call a no-holds barred approach, Neil.

I would gratefully accept half of the passion from you that Doug gives to the limbless in Virginia.

It's funny the way that you like to watch me dress. I didn't notice at first but then realised that you stare at me from the bed as I dress – starer! So now I dress more slowly. If it's sunny I move by the window. I choose the order in which I put on my clothes. You must like it or you wouldn't look so intensely. But, Neil, please tell me this: does that intensity equal passion?

Is it the passion demonstrated by Dorset Felt Roofing? Because you should know, they're the first for felt roofing in Weymouth and offer services that are unmatched in quality and reliability. Not only are they passionate about felt roofing in Dorchester and the surrounding areas, but they can offer a comprehensive range of services to boot. You can see that those old felt roofers have passion for roofing services hotly careering through every vein in their bodies.

I'd like to think the same goes for you, Neil, but I just don't know.

Neil, you once said that I was an angel. Well, that's just not good enough. Far too pure. I think that the depth of my passion makes me a Dark Angel.

I think that it's time for you to tell me about your passion…

Until then, with love—

No, with passion,

X

Written at the Merton College Masterclass, Oxford, in 2009, this piece by Neil Duffy became a Dark Angels legend. As a former COO of Interbrand, Neil debunked the misuse and vacuity of language that can often be associated with brand communication. Sadly Neil died in 2017 but his words live on to remind us of his wit and wisdom.

SONNET WITH LIGHTNING

MICHELLE NICOL

1. My Nana was full of superstitions. Never put new shoes on the table. If you spilled salt, throw a pinch over your left shoulder to fend off the devil. And a lone white feather was a sign that someone up there was watching you. 2. Her church was St Michael and All Angels. It was the place where I slid up and down the wooden floors as she hoovered the thick red carpets. 3. The last of the five Anderson sisters. She was the family history keeper. 4. She told me of her first love. The blond-haired boy on the bicycle. He took her to the Peak District where they dipped their feet in icy Dovedale and free-wheeled down the hills. 5. Married and widowed within a year. Letters from a sailor, praising the beauty of the Greek islands made it home from war. But he never did. 6. Years later, considering a second proposal, she prayed for guidance late into the night. In the darkness she was awoken by the sound of thunder. On opening the curtains, she saw a bolt of lightning split the air from heaven to earth, with a crack that made the windows rattle. Afterwards a still, dense quiet and dawn breaking. 7. She was sure it was a sign, but unsure what it meant. She asked her vicar for guidance. 'After the lightning came calm,' he said. So, just as her life had been split by the death of her first husband, it could continue in calm and security with a second. 8. Nana was ninety-two when she died. She'd celebrated St Patrick's day in Dublin with my sister and her great grandson. She only lived to the end of the month. 9. To see her sallow-skinned and frail in a hospital bed was a shock. We thought she was indestructible. 10. I returned north after that hospital visit. We all thought she'd rally round. She

knew she wasn't coming out. 11. There was a storm. The sky turned from copper pink to black. The power blinked off and I watched the lightning through my kitchen window. A single bolt split the air from heaven to earth. The room filled with a magnesium bright flare. The glasses rattled on the draining board, and then there was silence. 12. When the phone rang later that evening, I knew what the news would be. 13. I went to register her death with my mum. When asked the cause, the words would not come. I filled in the blank – cirrhosis of the liver. Not the final diagnosis anyone anticipated for a woman who baulked at the communion wine. 14. Returning to my car, I saw a white feather caught on the windscreen. I plucked it away before anyone noticed.

Written at Merton College, Oxford, in 2015, revised at Hawkwood House, the Cotswolds, in 2018. Michelle is a former journalist and a copywriter who has been through all levels of Dark Angels while developing her career as a brand storyteller.

LONDON TO BOMBAY 1939

FAYE SHARPE

Foreword

To my mother

I have come to understand that if I wish to accomplish something significant I must be prepared to ask for forgiveness rather than always to seek permission.

I have a vivid childhood memory. We all know what a liar memory can be but this one feels real to me. I was four or five years old and had committed some minor misdemeanour and got caught in the act of it. Giving me the opportunity to confess my sin, my mother asked me, 'Did you do that?' Obviously I had but I denied it and made up some excuse or other. She listened patiently and waited until I finished. 'Are you telling stories?' she asked. 'Telling stories' was my mother's euphemism for 'telling lies'. She was asking me, politely, if I was lying. I was. It is my very first memory of lying deliberately and lying became indelibly associated, in my impressionable child's mind, with telling a story. I learned a lesson that day, a hard one to unlearn. I still feel a frisson of that little girl's guilt every time I start to write. But my nature is to be a compulsive storyteller. There – I confess!

My mother was too. On dull afternoons when we were alone together and she was feeling rather low, I would ask her to tell me a story of the 'olden days' and she would enthral us both with stories of her wondrous, fabulous life in India, where she was born and where her grannies and their grannies lived and are buried. It was at the time I came to call 'B.C.', Before

180

Canada, before me. I knew that the stories were true, even if a little fanciful. Certainly, they were not lies. After both my parents died, I opened a box – 'Don't go rummaging in there!' – and found the maps, the route, my grandmother's diary, my grandfather's notes and photographs, so many photographs.

A story, well understood, gets closer to the heart of a person than any other way I know. Well told, a story provides a route to the truth hidden amongst the everyday, civil fibs of social intercourse and self-delusion – 'How are you?' 'Fine, thanks.' A story sifts through the facts and figures, the masks, the cover-ups, the veils of shame, bewilderment and embarrassment of the ordinary human doing to reveal the out-of-the-ordinary human being.

This story is an adventure story. It tells of how my mother's father, finding himself with his wife and two adolescent daughters in London mere weeks before the outbreak of the Second World War, decided that the only way to get his family home, back to the safety of India, was to drive seven thousand miles in a borrowed, fourth-hand, Ford sedan car!

In truth, this is a story of the beginning of the end; the end of the world as the world knew itself, the end of Britain as an empire on which the sun never set and the end of a family as it knew itself, embedded for generations in the economic, social and cultural roots of the sub-continent of India. It is a story of their race to cross borders before they closed, witnessing and getting caught up in the mass migrations of Europeans fleeing Hitler's advance, and it is also a reflection on the fact that a few short years later they too would be expelled, become European migrants and finally immigrants to a New World and a new life in Canada.

In telling this story I have trodden the shoreline between the dry lands of historical fact and evidential figures and the liquid worlds of memory, imagination and pure fiction. So, Mama.

181

Yes! This is me telling a story – one of yours in fact. And it's a whopper. Please forgive me.

Written after many Dark Angels experiences at Moniack Mhor, the Scottish Highlands; Aracena, Spain; Merton College, Oxford, and Hawkwood House, the Cotswolds; and now becoming a book. After many years of working life in the corporate world, Faye now says, 'I am a writer.'

AFTER LEARNING

THERESE KIERAN

What did you expect?[*]

— in Spain,
united old and new
faces in this place
of sweet podemos[*]

wrenched from the fold
for bold adventure
and unexpected pleasure
not always the angelic kind
still, something close enough

the yield of rough terrain
was tough on open toe,
for open I would surely go
with unsure guarantee
of delivery or task

I held my own;
given the tools – learned that rules
are mine to take, to bend, to break
And if a little Wabi-Sabi[*] should emerge
What next?

What might we expect?

Notes

What did you expect? references John Williams's book *Stoner*.

podemos – Spanish for 'we can/we are able'.

Wabi-Sabi – the Japanese craft that finds beauty in imperfection.

Written at Aracena, Spain, in 2015. Therese has been on several Dark Angels experiences that feed her creative work in Belfast as a designer and poet.

CREARE

ROWENA ROBERTS

creative (adj.), from create (v.) 'to bring into being', early 15c., from Latin creare 'to make, bring forth, produce, procreate, beget, cause'.

The Ego. A tattered, ill-fitting
cloak that covers the self,
carelessly stitched together from scraps of
survival and soul.

The Shadow. Safeguarder of secrets
and shame; reviled and despised,
it must at once exist and disperse
if we are to hold together, and make our selves whole.

The Soul. Gateway to the infinite divine
through which one, each one,
may grip and gather the glorious gold
that transcends time and unifies all.

Dark Angels. Compassionate conduits
of authentic creativity; creativity
which inspires consciousness and connection,
flowing as it does to and through the ego
from the shadow,
the soul,
our sacred pot of gold.

Written after Hawkwood House, the Cotswolds, in 2018. Rowena is a copywriter based in Manchester. She has been on Dark Angels courses at every level.

CAVELL STREET, LONDON. YEAR 5,679

ALEX FENTON

Once a Pole, now a yid.

Not for long, just glitch in life – it end one day. Then back to town of horse, a schlep from here, land of car and bus. Part of me left there – I feel not whole. I am golem; not dead, not alive...

Kvetch!?[1] Not me. Must keep shtum. Work and sell. Words come hard, but spiel come easy as weaving cloth. You understand?

Di Englender word 'alien' not a person, more... a paint. It wash off, but never erase – I am stuck in shtetl of their mind.

I am stuck, but once a Pole.

Centena written at Aracena, Spain, in 2018. Alex is a copywriter at me&dave, and he was intrigued by the centena form, first introduced as part of the 26 Armistice Project.

1. Yiddish for 'complain'/'whinge'.

THE MILLSTONE

SAM WEBB

I am, to most who pass, a lump of stone
With nothing more to tell than the mute trees.
And yet, compared to them, I've aeons known,
Whose secrets I might share with those I please.
Hands found me in the valley's sunken floor –
Less rough, less dexterous those than his that rent
Me from the rock, some thousand years before –
My bed, a Moorish mill, where might was spent.
With groans they hauled me uphill to La Finca
(How puny human labours make me smile)
Where I am now, useless, an idle thinker –
No chance of grist to grind for a long while.
So, idler, stay a time and dream my dreams
Of windmill sails and waterwheels in streams.

Sonnet written at Aracena, Spain, in 2018 following an exercise based on Shakespeare's sonnets. Sam had forged a glittering career at onefinestay, including stints in California. He is now thriving as a freelance writer and brand consultant.

FINDING A BRAVER WAY TO WORK WITH WORDS

BECCA MAGNUS

I don't know about you, but I find the average writing course or conference a bit trying. Sure, it's nice to be reminded of the basics, and to cover some niche material that perhaps we didn't know. But on average, a lot of it is foundational, and I personally don't feel the need to drop £500 to have my ego massaged. Saying all that, I'm keen to learn. I want to hone my craft. How do I do that without going to a session full to the brim with jargon and self-aggrandising bullshit? Dark Angels has an answer.

Dark Angels is not a course. It has no syllabus, no key learning objectives, no certificate at the end. Dark Angels is, instead, an invitation. A walled-off space, quite literally remote from the outside world, for you to explore.

In our lives, we create so many spaces for ourselves, but they often end up cramped, spaces that make us feel small, homogeneous and lacking. Within, we pursue our own nebulous concept of success, which inevitably involves narrow vision, the pursuit of success markers like awards over experimentation and curiosity, and a steely sense of competition. It's not conducive to real creativity.

Many say that in order to write, first you must create space. A physical space, a tiny corner of a room that is indisputably yours. A mental space, time carved out in an ever-changing, packed schedule to put pen to paper and to bring something new into the world. And an emotional space for you to say 'This is for me.' And it is absolutely OK if it's rubbish. Perhaps that is the hardest thing, the permission, not only to create, but to do it badly. It feels like such an indulgence that it must be good in order to be brought into the world.

Dark Angels invites you into a boundless space, where it's fine to be mediocre. You can write total crap and it's fine. All they ask is that you bring yourself to each writing task, and try. Say yes. See what happens. Bring a little bravery back to your writing practice.

How many times do we get permission from ourselves, from our clients, our bosses, our friends, to show up and try, even though what we produce might not be good? Rarely, if ever. Time demands quality, and if we cannot immediately produce something brilliant, we are rubbish. It's a false paradigm. Sometimes it takes being somewhere else, getting advice from a stranger, to realise that.

Basically, often our writing is a bit naff. It's fine. No one died because you wrote a crap sentence. Move on. Keep going.

At a Dark Angels retreat, essentially you do writing exercises. Lots of them. You open yourself up to discover what you can do with a single word or object. You explore. You engage with the world. You share with likeminded strangers. You come away a community. It's simple, it's brave and it's profound. It is strictly no bullshit. It is heavy with honesty, depth and personal stories, lovingly told. It's the best writing course I've ever done.

What can you expect? The unexpected. Arrive in a remote place. Open yourself to the world. Go somewhere unbidden, somewhere unique to you. A writing workshop that helps you do that? That's priceless. I can't wait to do my next course.

Becca Magnus wrote this after the Dark Angels foundation course at Loughcrew, Ireland, in 2018. She calls herself a joyful rebel, but also a freelance brand writer and graphic design dabbler. She won a Dark Angels scholarship for young writers.

Authors' biographies

NEIL BAKER

Neil is a writer and communications consultant with twenty-five years' experience of helping people tell their stories, share ideas and make connections. A D&AD pencil holder, he has won numerous other awards for his work with brands. His clients range from global consulting firms to small, grassroots charities. He is an Associate Poet with Canterbury's Wise Words Festival and a board member of writers' organisation 26. Neil also runs workshops in creativity and wellbeing through writing.

CLAIRE BODANIS

Claire has nearly twenty years' experience as a specialist in corporate reporting and sustainability communications. She set up Falcon Windsor in 2004 to do what she enjoys most: helping her clients communicate well through words. These include plcs such as ArcelorMittal, ASOS, Diageo, GKN and Tate & Lyle, as well as public-sector bodies like the BBC and the Cabinet Office. Today the Falcon Windsor team offers a full service from strategy and copywriting to digital and print production and delivery. Claire is co-author of the Dark Angels Collective novel, *Keeping Mum*.

GILLIAN COLHOUN

Gillian is a Belfast native who began her working life in London's publishing scene, but soon dived into the bracing waters of business writing, where she helps organisations tap into their unique stories. A university guest lecturer and mentor on brand- and writing-related programmes, she has guided over 300 companies through the cultural mind shifts of new identity programmes, content strategy and tone of voice. She is a regular speaker on the value of words in design and business.

STUART DELVES

Stuart has over thirty years' experience as a copywriter. Based in a sixteenth-century garret in Edinburgh's Old Town, he trades under the name Henzteeth. With the Arvon Foundation, then Bloom Reading Holidays, he ran over 130 residential courses. In 2005 Stuart initiated 26 Malts and in 2007 wrote *Creative Fire*, a book about Scotch the Brand. He's also a poet and an award-winning playwright. In 2014, after being Storyteller-in-Residence with Macsween of Edinburgh he brought his dramatist's skills to the service of his host client and wrote *Haggis Haggis Haggis* for the Edinburgh Fringe. Aside from Dark Angels he also runs Creative Retreats. Stuart is co-author of the Dark Angels Collective novel, *Keeping Mum*.

MIKE GOGAN

Mike is a writer, trainer and Dublin native, born under the shadow, shelter and shenanigans of the tower at Sandycove where James Joyce's *Ulysses* opens. A Dark Angel with the full clutch of courses under his belt, he has been writing to one audience or another, from one brand or another, for over twenty-five years. Day-to-day, as an in-house writer at Ireland's largest bank, he leads the change from bank language to customer language.

JAMIE JAUNCEY

Jamie has worked for many years with groups and organisations of all kinds on the power of language and stories to transform the way we see the world and our place in it. Jamie has published five novels – two of them shortlisted for the Royal Mail Scottish Children's Book of the Year Award – and has co-written with John Simmons *Room 121: A masterclass in writing and communication in business*. A former chairman of the Society of Authors in Scotland, he was for many years a director of the Edinburgh International Book Festival, the world's largest literary festival. He is also a musician and with his wife Sarah, a counsellor, runs personal development courses. Jamie is co-author of the Dark Angels Collective novel, *Keeping Mum*.

MARTIN LEE

Martin is Joint Managing Director of Acacia Avenue, an agency in Islington specialising in brand and marketing advice based on market research. Like many other Dark Angels, he's also a member of 26, and is one of its longest-serving directors. His lifelong passion for books and writing found professional expression in his former role as Marketing Director at Waterstones, and nowadays his pleasure is in writing for a life, rather than a living. Martin is co-author of the Dark Angels Collective novel, *Keeping Mum*.

ELEN LEWIS

Elen is a writer, editor and author. She writes novels about lightning and foundlings, books about brands (IKEA and eBay), eight ghost-written books that she can't talk about and poems in the V&A Museum and Welsh National Eisteddfod. She writes and runs workshops for clients like Sainsbury's, BP, DHL, Unilever and Diageo. She sits on the board of 26, to inspire a love of language, and is the editor of The Marketing Society. Elen is co-author of the Dark Angels Collective novel, *Keeping Mum*.

ANDY MILLIGAN

Andy is a founder of the business growth consultancy The Caffeine Partnership. A brand consultant since 1990, he has helped businesses around the world to define their brand promise and translate into words and actions what customers notice and value. Andy has published six business books and is co-author of the Dark Angels Collective novel, *Keeping Mum*. He has been a Plymouth Argyle fan since 1974, which has taught him invaluable life skills.

RICHARD PELLETIER

Richard began his writing life on a loud, hot summer's night in the ghetto, in a fit of inspiration, a pencil toss from the Baltimore home of H. L. Mencken, the great journalist and prose stylist. He writes for branding agencies and clients in the Pacific Northwest (his home) and beyond. With eleven fellow writers, he was a 2015 D&AD award-winner. Proud Dark Angel.

JOHN SIMMONS

John is an independent writer and brand consultant, formerly a director of Interbrand and Newell and Sorrell. His many books on writing for business include *We, Me, Them & It*, *The Invisible Grail*, *Dark Angels* and *26 Ways of Looking at a Blackberry*. With Jamie Jauncey he co-wrote *Room 121: A masterclass in writing and communication*. His fiction includes *The Angel of the Stories*, *Keeping Mum* (the Dark Angels Collective novel), *Leaves* and *Spanish Crossings*. His most recent novel *The Good Messenger* was published in 2018. He was awarded an Honorary Fellowship by Falmouth University for services to the creative industries. He is a founder director of 26.

CRAIG B. WATSON

Craig B. Watson used to be a writer and entertainer. Then he grew up and became the sort of lawyer they don't make TV dramas about. He's reasonably good at it too, provided you catch him after 10 a.m. It was doing a bit of legal 'sign-off' that led him to discover Dark Angels. He signed up to the courses and has since signed over his soul to the cause. He writes for business and for pleasure – some of it in his native Scots.

Acknowledgements

We all wish to thank our clients. The old cliché is true – without them this book would not have been possible. Particular thanks are due to those clients who are mentioned in the individual chapters, and for allowing us to feature work from their organisations and companies.

Special thanks to John Allert for writing the Foreword. John is a fine writer who is always welcome on Dark Angels courses whenever he can tear himself away from the fuel of Formula 1.

We're very grateful to the twelve writers who responded so brilliantly to our question: 'Why do you do what you do?' These are stars of the writing world who know Dark Angels well – and who know the ins and outs of writing from many different angles, as they demonstrate in their words on the section pages before each new chapter.

Our thanks are certainly due to the hundreds of writers who have attended Dark Angels courses over the years and who, by their presence and their words, have created the special character of Dark Angels. Among this group, we're especially grateful to the alumni who gave us permission to share the selection of work shown towards the back of this book. It was not easy making that selection. We could have printed an inspiring, big book of work written by Dark Angels. Perhaps one day we will.

Our thanks to Unbound for publishing this book. Our connection to Unbound is a Dark Angels one too. Founder John Mitchinson has attended Dark Angels courses at all levels and we remember him talking about the idea for Unbound at the Masterclass in Merton in 2011. Where else would we look for publishing support? Our views and values about books and language are shared. Unbound provides the platform for the supporters who subscribed generously to make sure this book happened – those patrons are listed at the front and back of the book, and we owe them a big Thank You. All books need supporters, and they certainly need readers.

At Unbound we loved working with John Mitchinson, Xander Cansell, Josephine Salverda, Sara Magness and the team around them including designers, editorial staff, marketing and printers. You've been great. For Dark Angels, Susanne Wakefield and Melissa Thom have kept our wings beating as we enter a new way of working.

Specific thanks go to Andy Henry (andyhenry.co.uk) for helping Gillian with her illustrations; and also to Rowan Adams, Sarah Dyson, Nicola Foster, Annie Heaton, Gill Hodge, Harriet Howey, Nicola Marsden and Jessica Rouleau, for their insights for Claire's chapter.

And naturally, there are personal thanks from each of the writers to their friends, family and clients who are such big parts of our lives.

Unbound is the world's first crowdfunding publisher, established in 2011.

We believe that wonderful things can happen when you clear a path for people who share a passion. That's why we've built a platform that brings together readers and authors to crowdfund books they believe in – and give fresh ideas that don't fit the traditional mould the chance they deserve.

This book is in your hands because readers made it possible. Everyone who pledged their support is listed at the front of the book and below. Join them by visiting unbound.com and supporting a book today.

Amina Ado
Douglas Aitken
Leonie Alexander
Melissa Bailey
Simon Bailey
Aidan Baker
Francesca Baker
Neil Baker
Jenny Barton
Claire Bodanis
Sophie Bodanis
Marc Boothe
Mark Britter
Charlotte Brookes
Christian Caron
Mathilde Caron
Monique Caron
Ross E. Chapman
Louisa Clarke
Martin Clarkson
Richard Cohen
Diego Contreras

Chris Corbett
Peter Cunningham
Davidovits Family
Olly Davy
Jan Dekker
Stuart Delves
Sophie Devonshire
Angela Dickson
Diverset Chartered Accountants
Guy Dresser
Deirdre Duff
Julius Falcon
Sarah Farley
Gary
Conor Gogan
Crea Gogan
Ina Gogan
Liam Gogan
Lorcan Gogan
Sarah Gogan
Mike Gogan
Sophie Gordon

Keith Gore
Roshni Goyate
Nicola Graham
Chrissie Grieve
Charlotte Halliday
Ann Hastie
Ashley Hayward
Daniel Herbert
Brian Hodges
Jill Hopper
Adrian Hornsby
Orla Houlihan
Ashley Hoyland
Andy Hyland
Charlotte Jane Berney
Jamie Jauncey
Sarah Jauncey
Wendy Jones
John Jordan
Deirdre Kearns
Naoimh Kenny
Howard Kyte
Stella Kyte
Martin Lee
Lindsay Lewandowski
Arthur Lewis Paynter
Rosie Lewis Paynter
Jo Liddell
Rebecca Magnus
Linda Marchant
Rosalyn McGregor
Henrietta McKervey
Katherine Mellor
Eck Mitchell
Jane Murton
Carlo Navato
Aoife Ni Chaoilte
Conor O'Donovan

Cate O'Kane
Richard Pelletier
Kath Penaloza
Ruth Petherick
Arthur Piper
Tom Potter
Bert Preece
Tim Rich
Lacy Rohre
Ada Simmons
Aimee Simmons
Jessie Simmons
Linda Simmons
Matt Simmons
Nicolas Sireau
Niamh Smithers
Matt Stephens
Pat Swaby
Melissa Thom
Rebecca Thomas
Simon Tobin
Paul Turnbull
Susanne Wakefield
Barry Watson
Corrie Watson
Irene Watson
Keith Watson
Lynsey Watson
Matt Watson
Leonardo Watson-Soto
Clare Weatherill
Sam Webb
Rob Williams
Joanna Wilmot
Isabel Windsor
Rebecca Windsor
Paul Zollinger-Read